KILTIE THE KINGMAKER

STEWART MAIDEN, CIRCA 1930.

KILTIE THE KINGMAKER

The Ten Lost Lessons of Bobby Jones's Teacher
Stewart Maiden

SIDNEY L. MATTHEW

SPORTS
MEDIA
GROUP

All inquiries should be addressed to:
Sports Media Group
An imprint of Ann Arbor Media Group LLC
2500 S. State Street
Ann Arbor, MI 48104

Printed and bound at Edwards Brothers, Inc., Ann Arbor, Michigan, USA

08   07   06   05   04   1   2   3   4   5

Library of Congress Cataloging in Publication data
Kiltie the kingmaker : the ten lost lessons of Stewart Maiden / Sidney L. Matthew,
editor.
        p. cm.
1. Maiden, Stewart. 2. Golfers—United States—Biography. I. Matthew, Sidney L.

     GV964.M34K55 2004
     796.352'092—dc22

                                        2004018334
ISBN 1-58726-108-1

To the man who knew Kiltie best,
his nephew James Cameron "Cam" Maiden, Jr.,
and to his grandson, Kiltie Leach,
and to Jim Tingley,
the historian of Nassau Country Club
where it all got started.

CONTENTS

FOREWORD

When Stewart Maiden became the golf professional at the Atlanta Athletic Club's East Lake Country Club, few people would have guessed that this diminutive, reticent Scot would play such a huge role in the history of golf. Stewart's people skills were somewhat lacking by today's standards. One time, when he was asked to give a lesson by furniture magnate J.J. Haverty, Stewart observed Haverty's swing on the practice tee and, after careful thought, observed, "My God, man, do you have to play golf?" Stewart later became the first man in history to use the line, "I suggest that you take a two week vacation from golf and then quit."

But what Stewart lacked in people skills, he made up with an absolutely graceful and powerful golf swing. His swing was grounded in the Carnoustie tradition, which was marked by an upright flowing motion and a syrupy smooth tempo. He also had a very simple but thorough understanding of the golf swing and knew how to communicate that information in a way that was easily absorbed by his students. His lessons tended to be short and to the point, with no wasted words either in instructional matters or in pleasant banter.

Within three decades of his arrival at East Lake, he would be known as "Kiltie the Kingmaker" for producing from the Athletic Club membership three national champions, Alexa Stirling, Charlie Yates, and my grandfather Bobby Jones. In addition to this, there were numerous players from the Athletic Club who achieved regional success. In fact, during the first three decades of the past century, no golf professional had as many successful students as did Stewart Maiden.

Much has been made of my grandfather's golfing success but one aspect of his game that is little known is that my grandfather never had a formal lesson from Maiden in his life. There would be times when Maiden would go to the practice tee to give my grandfather a pointer or two, but there never was an occasion where Maiden instructed my grandfather in the fundamentals of the game.

The same could not be said for my father, however. When my dad, Bob Jones III, was a teenager he decided to take up the game of golf in earnest. This alarmed my grandfather, who felt that the pressure of playing golf as Bobby Jones's son would be more pressure than my father could reasonably be expected to bear. My grandfather and Stewart developed a strategy that was designed to discourage my dad from trying to follow in his father's footsteps.

Bub (my family nickname for my grandfather) arranged for Stewart to give a private lesson to my dad at Peachtree Golf Club, which was under construction at that time in northeast Atlanta. Dad showed up at the range promptly at eight o'clock in the morning to find Stewart sitting under an umbrella on the practice tee, much in the same manner that Tommy Armour used to give lessons in Boca Raton, Florida. Unlike Armour, Stewart sat there without a smile and with only a bucket of brackish looking liquid at his side. "Start hittin' the ball, lad," was all Kiltie said. My dad started hitting shots, with Stewart making an occasional small correction. Finally, at about noon, my dad put down his club and started heading back toward the clubhouse. Maiden didn't move.

"Lad, where you goin'?" Maiden asked.

"I'm off to lunch, Stewart."

Maiden didn't miss a beat. "I don't take lunch. Get back here and keep hitting."

And so they continued with the lesson, my dad with sore hands and growling stomach, Stewart just with a growl. Finally at about 2:30 in the afternoon, my dad's hands began to bleed. He turned to Stewart, expecting sympathy. Instead, Stewart inspected his hands, pointed to the mysterious bucket, and said, "Stick 'em in there, lad. It'll toughen 'em up."

My father thrust his hands into a stinging bucket of brine. The bleeding in his hands stopped. He turned to Stewart, expecting relief, "What do I do now, Stewart?"

Maiden stared back at the young man, and said, "Keep hittin' the ball."

On the lesson went until late in the afternoon, but try as hard as he could to discourage him, Stewart Maiden could not help but teach my father the intricacies of the game. The next summer, my father won the City Amateur in Atlanta, and went on to compete in three national championships and numerous club and regional tournaments. At his peak, my father's handicap was +3, due in no small part, in his own words, to the lessons learned from "that damned Stewart Maiden."

If Stewart had lived today, he would be more famous than David Leadbetter and Butch Harmon. You would see his books everywhere and his presence on The Golf Channel would be ubiquitous. However, Stewart lived in a time when golf professionals lived much quieter, anonymous lives. What a treat and privilege to be given the insights into the golfing mind that created the pages in this book! Enjoy these pages and remember, "Keep hitting the ball!"

Robert T. Jones IV, Psy.D.
McDonough, Georgia
September 2003

PREFACE

O.B. KEELER

Stewart Maiden, golf professional at the East Lake course of the Atlanta Athletic Club, is known wherever the game is played as the teacher of Bobby Jones, Alexa Stirling, and Perry Adair, who, among them, have won more important golfing championships than the pupils of any other master the game has seen. Between them, Bobby Jones and Alexa Stirling have won all the major national championships in the United States—the National Open, the National Amateur, and the Women's National (Miss Stirling having held that title three times)—and also the Canadian Women's Championship. Two Women's Metropolitan Championships, two Women's Southern Championships, and five Southern Amateur Championships are among the other conquests of this unapproachable triumvirate. Certainly the methods of this little Scotsman from Carnoustie are to be regarded as distinguished—even distinctive.

No less distinctive is the teacher himself. Taciturn, of few words even for a Scot, Mr. Maiden has gone about his business with no ostentation whatever. All over America they call him "Kiltie the Kingmaker"— he is deservedly among the great authorities of the game. But that means nothing to "Kiltie." There is nothing he cares for less than the position of an authority. His supreme happiness is in the success of his pupils. Yet he does not talk much of them, and he talks less of golf, and of himself he talks not at all. It was with the utmost difficulty that he was persuaded to contribute a series of simple golf lessons to *Outdoor South,* a magazine of southern sports, of which this writer is editor, and a close friend of "Kiltie's." The attention attracted by these lessons was so remarkable and so general that it finally was arranged to publish a digest of the series in book form.

As one who has followed the devious ways of golf for nearly 28 years, I can commend these lessons to beginners in the game, and to duffers who have struggled with it more or less hopefully, and to players of every rank, even the best—for they are sure to be interested in the method and theories of the teacher who in one decade produced the two players regarded as the outstanding stylists not only of America but of the world—Bobby Jones and Alexa Stirling. It is an interesting if not a significant fact that in every lesson you may find some reference to Bobby Jones's—"Bob Jones," his teacher always calls him—pet manner of executing a shot, or some trick of style characteristic of the master-stylist of modern times. In those references, if you read a bit between the lines, you may gain a hint of the deep affection existing between teacher and pupil; between the champion-maker and the champion; concealed though it be among the abrupt and business-like phrases of the silent little Scot, who, in my opinion, comes as near as any man living to knowing the truth about that most puzzling of all sporting sciences—the game of golf. Perhaps as well as anyone I realize what Stewart Maiden has done for golf in America, and this little book of lessons is by no means an unimportant contribution. Brief and terse and amazingly direct, it is a good expression of Stewart Maiden himself. I could accord it no higher praise or warmer commendation.

EAST LAKE MEMORIES

CHARLIE YATES

As long as I can remember, Stewart Maiden has been a household name in my family's home. I was born on Fourth Street in Atlanta in 1913. My father, Pressley Daniel Yates, and my mother, Julia Richardson Yates, moved to 307 Second Avenue, SE, in 1914. That street was significant because it divided the No. 1 and later No. 2 courses of beloved East Lake. You could say the Yates family lived smack dab in the middle of East Lakes Links. My father was an avid golfer sporting a 23 handicap. He was left-handed but that did not deter him from capturing the East Lake One Day Medal Handicap Tournament with a net 62.

Like my father, I was a left-handed lad. I was given an old sawed-off left-handed mashie with which I "tore up the lawn." My father loved every minute of it down to the detail that I slept with my first set of juvenile clubs.

Before long, I was slipping across the street on Second Avenue to see what was happening. I saw this fellow named Bob Jones who was the rising star. My good friend Berrien Moore and I were bold enough to go up to Bob Jones and see what he was about. To our delight, he was very kind to us. He spent some time talking to us, took us into the locker room, and even gave us some of his golf balls and a taste of that great elixir of Atlanta called Coca-Cola. We thought we had arrived. It was the beginning of a friendship that lasted until Bob passed in 1971.

The pro at East Lake was the legendary Scotsman Stewart Maiden. Stewart was quite dour and matter of fact in his demeanor. He was a wonderful, wonderful little fellow. Many people called him Kiltie. Have you ever heard of that? I had the greatest respect for Stewart, although I was too young really to take any lessons from him. Stewart had two great prodigies with whom he worked. One was Bob Jones and the other was Alexa Stirling who had won the Women's Championship and she was a little older than Bob. They played as youngsters together. I had the greatest admiration for Alexa although I didn't know her as well as I did Bob.

I used to walk along behind Bob and watch him play. He never practiced much. You had to see him play if you wanted to see him in action.

We used to see Stewart around the club. Sometimes we saw him with Bob. It wasn't long before I came under the watchful eye of "Kiltie." Kiltie noticed my dogged determination and told my dad that I had the foundation for a good golfer. My father felt pretty good about that because he wanted to find something that would keep me occupied and out of boyish mischief.

Even with these kind words of encouragement, Stewart Maiden told my father that he was starting me out wrong with a left-handed club. That is when my dad went to purchase a right-handed set of clubs with a little Scottish tartan bag from a department store. To give you an idea of how big I was then, the clubs measured 18 inches. With my new right-handed clubs, I attacked the game with renewed vigor. I won the first cup at age 11 when I finished on top of the first flight of the city junior tournament.

Stewart Maiden was there for some of Bob Jones's most poignant moments. So was I. For instance, in 1925 Bob was defeated in the U.S. Open Championship contested at Worster, Massachusetts. When Jones returned home I told him, "I'm sorry you lost." Bob shot back, "Don't worry about it son, you never really know who your friends are until you lose."

In 1926 I was privileged to travel on the special train that carried many Atlantians to New York for the historic first ticker tape parade and celebration for Bob. The train was called the "Bobby Jones Special." When Bob's ship the Aquatania arrived, I squeezed through the crowd to see Mayor Jerry Walker and an entourage of celebrities. Suddenly a policeman grabbed me by my collar. "Hold on buddy," the cop told me. "You don't belong in that picture." I pulled my jacket lapel around for him to see my ribbon announcing "Welcome Bobby Jones." I told the cop, "I'm on the committee. I reckon I do belong in the picture." The cop smiled and told me, "Sure you do. Get on over there with you."

East Lake was a wonderful place for young boys and girls to grow up. We were lucky to have someone like Kiltie Maiden to help us with our golf games.

ACKNOWLEDGMENTS

The research required to complete this book was made much easier with the help of many people and clubs whose assistance is gratefully acknowledged.

Much of the biographical information of Kiltie's life was generously supplied by his brother's son and Kiltie's nephew, James C. "Cam" Maiden. Cam spent hours sharing his insights with the author and provided photos of the family. Cam knew Kiltie from his visits to Glen Cove and Nassau Country Club, and is one of the few living links to Kiltie.

Kiltie's grandson, "Kiltie" Leach, was also most helpful with various details and anecdotes. The historian of Nassau Country Club, Jim Tingley, was especially helpful in supplying photographs and connections of the Maiden brothers to Nassau Country Club, East Lake Golf Club, and to the Alex Smith clan.

Alex Smith's granddaughter Joan Hammond also provided photos and family details.

We are also grateful to Nassau Country Club, East Lake Country Club, Carnoustie Golf Club, Caledonia Golf Club, Peachtree Golf Club, and Hillerich and Bradsby Company who granted permission to reprint catalogues, golf tip brochures, and photographs of Kiltie when he was employed by them.

Tommy Barnes of East Lake also got a valuable lesson from Kiltie. Kiltie told Tommy how to play a wee pitch by feel. "It should feel like you are turning and putting your left hand in your right rear trouser pocket," Kiltie said.

Charlie Yates should be specially thanked for his memories of East Lake and about Kiltie also. And the relatives of O.B. Keeler including Dr. Bill Hedrick and Mary Ella Ackerly permitted your author to research the helpful archives of O.B. Keeler.

Peggy Morton of Highlands and Bob Jones's law partner, Arthur Howell, also supplied stories about Kiltie Maiden giving golf lessons to them and others at East Lake.

A few friends deserve to be mentioned in memoriam because I took so long compiling the information that they didn't live to see the book. Watts Gunn knew Kiltie well at East Lake and shared many humorous stories; Woodrow Bryant learned the club maker's art from Kiltie at East Lake; Charlie Brett of Nassau Country Club caddied for Bobby Jones at Nassau and passed along the true story of Jones's Calamity Jane putter; Jimmy Hosie caddied for Jones in 1927 at Carnoustie following Jones's successful defense of his Open Championship title. Jimmy lived at 22 Tennis Road in Carnoustie and hosted your author for tea in 1989 and 2000.

Finally, grateful appreciation is extended to my faithful staff, Gwynne Chason and Cindy Thompson, for help on the manuscript and the prepress drudgery.

My wife, Linda, and son, Geoffrey, and daughters, Lauren and Jennifer, can exhale now that this book is finally done.

To God Be the Glory,
Sidney L. Matthew
Tallahassee

THE LIFE OF STEWART MAIDEN

SIDNEY L. MATTHEW

A picture is worth a thousand words. That is why Stewart Maiden was so prolific in his time. Stewart Maiden never said much but he spoke volumes. Kiltie behaved as though actions spoke louder than words. Perhaps that is why he was misunderstood as overly dour. Just the image of his golf swing was so vivid in the minds of his famous students that it spoke to them. And later the deeds of Kiltie's students sang in the record books for succeeding generations to the tune of 17 major championships.

The Silent Scot

Bobby Jones was one lad who heard Maiden loud and clear although Stewart never spoke to him. Instead, young Jones became mesmerized by shadowing Maiden around the East Lake Golf Club and watching him swing. In those days Jones had nothing on his mind but his cap. But he ran like the wind back to the "mulehouse" where he stayed and practiced what was burned into his mind's eye.

That's not to say that Stewart Maiden never spoke at all. He did, but it was with such economy of phrase that only a few words translated into entire volumes of golf instruction. "Shoot the works" was Kiltie's philoso-

A YOUTHFUL STEWART MAIDEN
PRIOR TO HIS VOYAGE TO AMERICA IN 1908.

phy of golf. By this he meant to warn the player against the policy of playing safe to protect a lead. "Try for all ye got, because when yer down there's nothing else to do. It doesn't take any brains then to try for everything. To that extent the man who is down has the advantage of the man who is up. He's on a one-way street. Shoot the works. That's all there is to do."

To Kiltie there was no such entity as a safe lead. A safe lead was when the opponent stuck out his hand to congratulate you as the winner of the match.

"The idea in match golf is to get a man down and then to get him farther down. When you are one up, try to be two up on the next hole. When you have him nine down, try to get him ten down. Play to win every hole, right up to the stage when you may be compelled to play for a half, and then try to stick one up there for a single putt. Play for your best shot, not your safest."

In Kiltie's limited vocabulary the word *safe* was not employed to describe the proper play of golf. "I think that when a regular golfer plays safe deliberately, down in his system somewhere there's a sense of guilt whether he knows it or not. And I think that guilty feeling smears a lot of shots and breaks up a lot of matches and tournaments where the man on top is playing what he thinks is a safe game. Let him play all he has and try for his best shots. That's the way to get them."

Kiltie had walked a few miles in the cleats of the great player. Born in Carnoustie, Scotland, Kiltie was the best player around after Alex Smith came over to find his fame and fortune. Carnoustie manufactured the greatest number of golfing professionals who ventured to America. Three hundred. Even more than St. Andrews. And the Carnoustie boys won their fair share of the honors too. Alex Smith won two U.S. Open Championships in 1906 and 1910. His brothers didn't play too badly either. Brother Willie Smith won the Open in 1899 at Baltimore Country Club. Willie finished second twice (1906, 1908); Alex three times (1898, 1901, 1905). Both Alex and Willie each lost a play-off too. McDonald lost the play-off for the Open title in 1910 and is considered the greatest player never to win a major. He lost the British Open at Hoylake in 1930 second only to Bob Jones. He also was bridesmaid to Jones in the U.S. Open contested at Interlachen that same year.

Carnoustie turned out great golfers with the machine-gun precision that army gunners used to practice their skills on the firing range in earshot of the Barry Burn on the Old Course. When Stewart left for America's shores in 1908, "There was no one in the coons" as great a player as he. Kiltie played off plus 1.

3

JAMES CAMERON MAIDEN SR. AND HIS WIFE
ALISON. STEWART MAIDEN IS SITTING ON HIS
FATHER'S KNEE AND JAMES MAIDEN JR. IS STANDING
TO HIS MOTHER'S LEFT.

The Maiden Family

James Cameron Maiden Sr. was the patriarch of the
family. Standing about 5' 6", he wore a full bushy beard
that would have rivaled that of Old Tom Morris. His
warm, twinkling eyes and ready smile especially stand
out in a photograph taken with his wife at their home
whose address was 93 Dundee Street. Mr. Maiden was
born in 1842 and died August 4, 1914 before the war to
end all wars. He was an unusually bright man and rose
to the white-collar position of head payroll clerk at the

JAMES CAMERON MAIDEN SR. AND ALISON
MAIDEN, STEWART'S PARENTS, AT THEIR HOME IN
CARNOUSTIE, SCOTLAND.

foundry in Carnoustie. He was not a golfer. His wife,
Alison, was also small and sturdy in stature and dispo-
sition. She was a dominant force in any issue and her
opinions carried great weight and authority. Seven children were born of the marriage, three boys and four
girls. Each of the boys became golf professionals, James,
Stewart, and Allan. The four girls were Francis (Fannie),
Alison (Elsie), Jessie, and Minnie (she went to Australia). Jessie became the wife of another Carnoustie golf
professional, Alex Smith. On the cobbles, as a barefoot
boy in wee "kilties," Stewart batted homemade cork balls

with improvised sticks and acquired the nickname "Kiltie," which stuck to him ever since. James, known as "Jimmy," was an unusually stable member of the family. Like his father, Jimmy was the class leader in his school and also was awarded the prize for general knowledge and regular attendance from the Barry Public School. Jimmy and his brother were avid golfers and each perfected the "Carnoustie" swing. The "free pivot" principally distinguished the swing from the style of players at St. Andrews. The Carnoustie players kept their feet close together when driving and also got their shoulders "grandly through" by allowing the head to move back from the point of address. They employed a long smooth swing characterized by a forceful drive of the hips forward with the hands held high, producing a characteristic draw on the shots.

Brother Allan emigrated to Australia and was the longtime professional at Victoria Golf Club in Melbourne. One of his students was Peter Thomson, five times winner of the British Open.

In 1901 20-year-old Jimmy Maiden emigrated as the assistant to Alex Smith at Nassau Country Club, Long Island. Three years later, in 1904, Jimmy became head professional at Youngstown, Ohio Country Club. He later took the helm at Inverness Club in Toledo, Ohio. His next position was in 1906 as head professional at East Lake Golf Club in Atlanta.

Jimmy was a superb player. He tied for third in the 1906 U.S. Open and placed second in the 1905 Western Open. He won the Ohio State Open in 1906 and the Eastern PGA in 1908 against a field loaded with big names and held at Garden City. Jimmy's swing was truly beautiful to behold. He actually won a gold medal for "the finest swing in golf" in a contest on the roof of the Astor Hotel in New York City on December 21, 1914.

ALEX SMITH WAS THE FIRST GOLF PROFESSIONAL AT THE EAST LAKE GOLF CLUB. SMITH WON TWO U.S. OPEN CHAMPIONSHIPS, IN 1906 AND 1910. HIS BROTHER WILLIE SMITH WON THE OPEN IN 1899 AND FINISHED SECOND TWICE (1906 AND 1908). ALEX'S BROTHER MCDONALD SMITH LOST THE PLAY-OFF FOR THE OPEN TITLE IN 1910 AND IS CONSIDERED THE GREATEST PLAYER NEVER TO WIN A MAJOR. HE LOST THE BRITISH OPEN AT HOYLAKE IN 1930, SECOND TO BOB JONES. ALEX SMITH MARRIED STEWART MAIDEN'S SISTER JESSIE.

ALEX SMITH AT THE BELLEVIEW BELLAIR GOLF CLUB IN CLEARWATER, FLORIDA, CIRCA 1926.

ALEX SMITH, JESSIE MAIDEN SMITH, AND DAUGHTER FRANCES. JESSIE MAIDEN SMITH WAS AN OLDER SISTER OF STEWART AND JIMMY MAIDEN.

IN 1902, 20 YEAR OLD JIMMY MAIDEN IMMIGRATED AS
THE ASSISTANT TO ALEX SMITH AT NASSAU COUNTRY
CLUB, LONG ISLAND. JIMMY WAS THE SECOND HEAD
PROFESSIONAL AT THE EAST LAKE GOLF CLUB IN
ATLANTA. JIMMY WON THE OHIO STATE OPEN IN 1906
AND THE EASTERN PGA IN 1908. HE WON A GOLD
MEDAL FOR THE "FINEST SWING IN GOLF" AT A CONTEST
ON THE ROOF OF THE ASTOR HOTEL IN NEW YORK
CITY ON DECEMBER 21, 1914. AT AGE 43, JIMMY WON
THE LONG ISLAND OPEN CHAMPIONSHIP IN 1924 AT
ST. ALBANS GOLF CLUB.

At age 43 Jimmy won the Long Island Open Championship in 1924 at St. Albans Golf Club.

His brother-in-law Alex Smith was head professional at East Lake when he arrived. It wasn't long before Jimmy's skills in organizing and operating an efficient golf club were properly recognized by everyone. Indeed, Jimmy was a founding member of the U.S. PGA while brother Allan was a founding member of the Australian PGA.

Kiltie Comes to America

In 1908 Jimmy was called to become head professional at Nassau Country Club in Long Island, New York. He encouraged his younger brother Stewart to recognize that there were plenty of opportunities for aspiring golf professionals in the United States. Stewart rose to the challenge. There was a small celebration for Stewart by his friends before he set out on the journey:

> A largely attended meeting of members of Carnoustie Golf Club was held in the clubhouse last night to give a send-off to Stewart Maiden, one of their leading players, who leaves this week for America, having adopted professionalism. The club secretary presented Mr. Maiden with a handsome steamer trunk and expressed the regret of the members at losing so excellent a player, but wished him a prosperous career in America. Orchestral selections were given during the evening by Messrs. David Crabbe (piano), David McKay (violin) and Fred Japp (cornet). Songs were rendered by Messrs. Wm. Lawson, Thomas Ogg, George Swankie, Fred Brand and others.

Although it has been widely reported that Kiltie came straightaway to East Lake to replace his brother

AT THE NASSAU COUNTRY CLUB *(LEFT TO RIGHT)*, ALEX SMITH, GEORGE LOWE, WILLIE ANDERSON, AND STEWART MAIDEN.

Jimmy, actually Stewart initially accepted a job as head professional of the Wee Burn Country Club in Darion, Connecticut during 1908. In fact, the *Golfers Annual* lists Kiltie as professional of Wee Burn in 1908. Later that year, Stewart arrived at East Lake to spell Jimmy.

Young Bobby Jones remembered first setting eyes on "Kiltie." "Stewart was just another little Scot, like Jimmy, only Scotcher! There was nothing sensational about him. He said very little and I couldn't understand a single word of what he said."

"Jimmy and Dad and Mother did the talking, and I wondered at first if Stewart could talk at all," recalled Jones.

Stewart became a colorful personality at East Lake and the members soon began to exchange stories about Stewart's teaching methods.

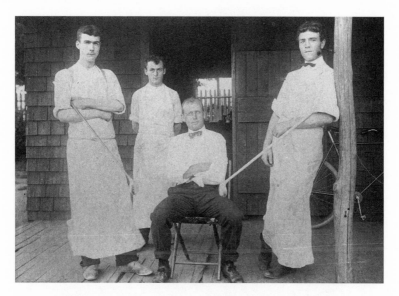

THIS IS A SCENE AT THE NASSAU COUNTRY CLUB PRO SHOP, CIRCA 1907. *(LEFT TO RIGHT)* JIMMY MAIDEN, DICK CLARKSON, ALEX SMITH, AND FRED LOWE.

Bob Jones chronicled some of these.

"Stewart was a real funny guy. He had a talent for making very pungent irreverent, witty remarks and I remember several instances in which he commented on members in one way or another. Of one of them he said, not wholly seriously, 'Oh, he's a great player. He only has one fault; he can't hole out soon enough.'"

When asked how Stewart was coming along teaching another member, he answered in his thick Scottish brogue, "I can't do a thing for him—after five minutes, he's teaching me."

Still a third member sought help from Kiltie when his game had deserted him. Usually Kiltie asked the member to hit half a dozen shots, and he obliged. As the member addressed yet another ball, Kiltie intervened, grabbed the player's wrist with his trademark

STEWART "KILTIE" MAIDEN AT CARNOUSTIE, SCOTLAND.

iron grip and looked at him eye-to-eye: "Dammit, Red, do you *have* to play golf?"

Kiltie's advice on one occasion has often been repeated on courses throughout the country. "The best thing for you to do is lay off the game for two weeks, then quit altogether."

"He was just that way," Jones observed, "if you did not have any particular promise, he'd give you lessons all right, but he wouldn't take much interest in you."

Bob Jones's law partner Ralph Williams took a lesson from Maiden at East Lake on a bright Saturday morning. The lesson was going smoothly when Ralph's curiosity about golf theory got the best of him. "Kiltie," Ralph asked, "I see what you're saying up to the point of hitting the ball. What about the proper position of the hands and arms after that?" Kiltie didn't even stop to think before he shot back. "I don't give a damn what you do after you hit the ball, Mr. Williams, cause it really doesn't matter now, does it?"

Kiltie and Alexa

Not long after Kiltie arrived at East Lake, he met the British consul in Atlanta, Dr. Alex W. Stirling. Born in Peebles, Scotland, Dr. Stirling graduated from Edinburgh University around 1880. He was trained in the medicine of the ears, eyes, nose, and throat (EENT) but later specialized in conditions of the eyes. Wanderlust took Dr. Stirling the long way around to Atlanta. First he traveled as the ship's doctor to Buenos Aires with his wife and first daughter Janet. From there he went to Denver and gradually worked east to Chicago and New York. After doing graduate work in New York, Dr. Stirling settled in Atlanta. Dr. Stirling lived in a comfortable English-style cottage home across the street from the 10th tee. A slender man with red whiskers and wire-rimmed spectacles, Dr. Stirling was a keen and canny Scot whose fervent hopes focused upon his young daughter Alexa. O.B. Keeler observed, "Character and determination stood out all over Dr. Stirling. That's where gallant little Alexa got her foundation for competitive golf." Alexa was a lithe red-haired, freckle-faced girl who was three years older than "Little Bob" Jones. She was a talented violinist but her music did not prevent young Alexa from playing golf with the other youngsters at East Lake. Kiltie quipped that if Alexa

ALEXA STIRLING, ABOUT AGE 20, IN FRONT OF THE EAST LAKE CLUBHOUSE. ALEXA WON THE AMERICAN WOMEN'S AMATEUR CHAMPIONSHIP THREE YEARS IN A ROW (1916, 1919, 1920). THE TOURNAMENT WAS NOT PLAYED DURING WWI.

ALEXA STIRLING FRASER

"would only leave that dashed fiddle alone, she would make a great golfer." Whereas Bob Jones never took a formal golf lesson, Alexa was taken under the close tutelage of Kiltie Maiden. Kiltie imbued each fundamental aspect of the golf swing into his young pupil. The genius of that skill combined beautifully with her uncommon courage and character. The result was one of the most remarkable records in all of women's golf.

While Little Bob Jones was shadowing Maiden on casual matches on the links, Alexa practiced her violin and her golf. Alexa's first competition was not particularly a lesson in equity, however. Mrs. Mary Bell Meador was landlady for the Jones family during their first summer at East Lake. A small 3-inch golf cup was put up as a prize by Mrs. Meador to be played for by the neighborhood kids over six holes at old East Lake. She must have believed her six-year-old son Frank might have an even chance to win that cup along with Perry Adair and Alexa. She was mistaken. The lowest score was probably returned by Alexa, the only girl in the field. But when young Frank tallied up the scores, either his arithmetic or manners had a bad day. Frank determined Little Bob was the champion no matter what the scores showed. Mrs. Meador proudly presented the cup. It was the last occasion on which Alexa was not recognized as rightful champion of the links. Bob Jones confessed years later, "I'd love to go over that round of six holes again and check it up. Because I'll always believe Alexa won that cup."

As Kiltie and the golfing world soon learned, the willowy Alexa proved to be very coachable. The key to Kiltie's style was simplicity itself. Not one to promote a "mechanical swing," Kiltie believed that "too many maxims in golf instruction only confused pupils." "Of course, you cannot think of all these things during a stroke," Kiltie reminded his pupils. "Just take the club back and swing the club through."

Alexa traveled to Nassau Country Club in Glen Cove, Long Island in 1914 to play in her first U.S. Women's Amateur Championship. She was then 17. Although she lost in the first round that year, Alexa survived to the semifinals of the 1915 Amateur. And she won both the 1915 Women's Southern Amateur and the Druid Hills Invitational in Atlanta.

Maiden's students broke through big in 1916 to make golf history. Alexa won the first of her three consecutive amateur titles at Belmont Springs Country Club in October at Waverly, Massachusetts. That was O.B. Keeler's first chance to see her, too: "The ladies used to say her father, Dr. Stirling, 'jinxed' her by attending the tournaments and popping out from behind trees when he was supposed not to be in the gallery. Anyway, as in the case of Bobby Jones, she didn't win a big one until her father gave up following her."

Red Cross Matches

The next year championship golf was suspended during World War I. Kiltie's pupils used the time wisely playing in a series of matches against amateurs and professionals for the benefit of the Red Cross. Alexa and Bobby were joined by Elaine Rosenthal and Perry Adair, the first "Kid Wonder from Dixie." Perry earned his title by twice winning the Southern Amateur Championship.

These kids had the time of their lives traveling across the country playing golf while wealthy patrons paid large sums for the privilege of caddying for the stars. They raised over $150,000 in the worthwhile effort. During an 1918 exhibition at Wannamoissett Club in

THE DIXIE WHIZ KIDS *(FRONT, LEFT TO RIGHT)* PERRY ADAIR AND BOBBY JONES. GEORGE WASHINGTON ADAIR, PERRY'S FATHER, STANDING BEHIND.

Rhode Island, a tall 15-year-old girl named Glenna Collett was in the gallery. Rosenthal shot 80 for a new course record and Alexa's iron play was equally impressive to the young spectator. Collett was so inspired she took lessons from Alex Smith and began a career of her own. She would go on to win six Women's Amateur Championships and establish new frontiers for women's golf.

During the war Alexa served as a lieutenant in the Women's Motor Corps. After the war she continued her golfing legend by successfully defending the Women's

Amateur title at Shawnee-on-Delaware. The *Atlanta Journal* applauded the effort:

> Eastern cities were amazed by the power and skill of her game. Almost to a man they agreed that no other women in the world, with the possible exception of Miss Leitch, the English champion, could compare with her. This year they must be even more of the opinion for never has Miss Stirling played so well. Not one man in a hundred can drive as far. Her tee shots average over two hundred yards; her irons are played accurately and with fine distance; her approaching when she is at the top of her game is almost faultless; and her putting seldom fails. Miss Stirling has in the highest degree the two qualities that go to make up a champion—skill plus courage.

Few people knew that Alexa, like Bob Jones, was just a weekend golfer. So the correctness of her fundamentals learned from Kiltie must have been astounding. Neither Alexa nor Bobby usually touched a club from October to April. Then in 1920 Alexa accomplished a feat Bobby Jones was never able to pull off—a third consecutive Amateur championship at Mayfield Country Club in Cleveland. Jones had two chances, too, but he never could equal this challenge. Keeler saw Alexa make history:

> Miss Stirling won the Women's Championship for the third consecutive time with the finest golf I ever saw a woman display. I think at Mayfield she reached close to the limits of feminine golfing ability in her match with Ms. Vanderbeck, when she set a new course record with an 80 from the regular tees.

Keeler was astounded as he watched Alexa outdrive her opponents from 10 to 40 yards until the last hole,

IN MAY 1920, ALEXA STIRLING WAS THE REIGNING
NATIONAL WOMEN'S AMATEUR GOLF CHAMPION. SHE
IS SEEN HERE DRIVING A TRACTOR AND BREAKING THE
FIRST GROUND FOR THE NEW MUNICIPAL GOLF CLUB AT
PIEDMONT PARK IN ATLANTA.

when the difference was 60 yards! He flatly said "no
such prodigious hitting had ever been done by any
woman golfer in America." Keeler beamed:

> To me no woman golfer who ever lived can compare with
> the Alexa who won three championships in a row and
> whom I never saw beaten before the semifinal round.
> There was the finest iron player the feminine world of
> golf ever saw; there was the true replica of Stewart
> Maiden.

Alexa went to the finals in 1923 but came up short despite the exhortations of her mentor. Keeler reported:

> Stewart Maiden who knows more about Miss Stirling's golf than anybody else including herself said after the close match with Miss Burns that it looked as if Miss Stirling had lost her nerve. He gave her a lecture before the next round and she stepped out with a fine round and won easily.
>
> The Atlanta girl simply was not right. In amazing contrast to the bold and decisive game of three years ago she seemed trying to play safe, playing as if trying not to lose a hole instead of going out to win it. . . . Miss Stirling was shockingly loose with her approaches where her firmness used to rival that of the best professionals. In the long game she was good enough. Near and on the greens she lacked confidence and touch. This induces the conclusion that it really was nerves.

In fact Maiden's star protégée would conquer her nerves and go on to win two Canadian Women's Amateur championships in 1920 and 1934. She also reached the finals of the U.S. Amateur in 1925 and the finals of the Canadian Amateur in 1922 and 1925.

In surveying his contributions to Alexa's career, Maiden summed up: "I taught Miss Alexa Stirling almost from the beginning of her study of golf and she, too, has done very well. Perhaps this indicates that my method is sound."

"Bobby Jones's Doctor"

Kiltie Maiden's skill with the perfected Carnoustie swing was not lost on young Bobby Jones either. Jones "shadowed" Kiltie all over the East Lake Course. They never talked to each other. But after Bobby had gotten

MASTER BOBBY JONES WITH MENTOR STEWART
MAIDEN. JONES IS APPROXIMATELY AGE 15.

an eyeful after four or five holes, he ran back to the
little "mulehouse" by the 13th green and practiced a
capful of balls with a sawed-off cleek given him by Fulton
Colville, whose name in history is indelibly inscribed
for that single generous act. Before long, even the experts could not tell Maiden and Jones apart. One of
Stewart Maiden's old friends watched Bobby driving off
during a Southern Amateur tournament in Birming-
ham. He insisted that Stewart Maiden was the young
lad. "Sorry," he was told, "Stewart's not here." The man
was adamant, "Oh, yes he is! Do you think I don't recognize that old Carnoustie swing? Nobody else in the

world hits a golf ball like that!" Not only did Jones copy Stewart Maiden's swing, but he also imitated other bizarre swings by members of East Lake Golf Club. Young Bobby could entertain the adults for hours reproducing the bizarre movements of judges, doctors, and lawyers struggling to play the game.

Kiltie's first impression of Little Bob Jones was that of a serious little fellow with an abnormally large head and a thin body. "And the first time I ever saw him hit the ball, I recognized as fine a golf swing as I had ever seen. And Bobby wasn't over 7 then." "Stewart Maiden," said Jones later, "had the finest and soundest style I had ever seen. Naturally I did not know this at the time, but I grew up swinging like him." Maiden was of the old-fashioned Scottish school of thought that advocated the old maxim that the left hand should be regarded as the master hand in the swing. "Give it the back of the left hand" was his way of encouraging a smooth follow-through so as to bring the hands more or less to the level of the left ear. O.B. Keeler delighted in chronicling the characteristic details of Maiden's style:

> Almost square stance, feet very close together; hands held low and close to his knickers; right hand more on top of the club than any other crack golfer; upright, compact swing; the ball nearly opposite the left heel for normal full shots and nearly off the right heel for his famous knock down or push shot.

Whenever young Jones got into trouble, Stewart could usually diagnose the problem in an instant. Bob's most common mistake, if the only one, was playing the ball too far back in his stance. "Move the ball up," Stewart would say, "Now knock hell out of it!" By the time Jones had finished his follow-through, Maiden was walking back to the clubhouse. He already knew the boy was cured.

FROM LEFT TO RIGHT, JIMMY MAIDEN, BOBBY JONES, BOBBY CRUICKSHANK, AND STEWART MAIDEN. THIS PICTURE WAS TAKEN JUST BEFORE THE PLAY-OFF IN 1923 FOR THE U.S. OPEN CHAMPIONSHIP CONTESTED AT INWOOD COUNTRY CLUB.

Jones went through seven lean years in which he never won a major championship. On the way to his first major victory at Inwood in 1923, Kiltie was concerned: "Why, he's not out hitting me off the tee very much. He's hitting the shots very well but the old kick isn't there."

Bob's wooden shots simply weren't getting the range he was used to. Then Stewart Maiden suggested that he swing his hands a bit more and restrict the pendulum motion of his wrists. Keeler even sat on the ground trying to trace the path of Bob's driver to see what was the matter. He saw that the club "swept the turf in a straight line 14 inches before turning off and up and with his heels 13 inches apart and a definite loop from the inside out." It wasn't long before Maiden straightened the boy out.

Beginning in 1923 Jones learned a valuable "secret" which led him on the road to seven fat years and 13 major championships. Many years later he shared his "secret" with the father of another great champion of the modern era—Jack Nicklaus. Jack's father later told his son about the "most helpful piece of advice I received from Bob." Jones said:

> I think I was a fairly good young golfer, but I never became what I would call a really good golfer until I had been competing for quite a number of seasons. You see, when I first started to play in the big tournaments, whenever anything went wrong, I'd run home to Stewart Maiden, our pro at East Lake. Finally, I matured to the point where I understood my game well enough to make my own corrections during the course of a tournament, and *that's* when I'd say I became a *good* golfer.

The advice had an important impact upon Nicklaus since he, too, had been "running home" to his teacher, Jack Grout, for quick fixes to his swing. Jones's advice made Nicklaus "more determined to learn everything I could about my swing so that, to some extent, I could diagnose my own errors and put myself back on my game. I cannot tell you what a big factor this is in tournament play. It may be the biggest factor of all in shaping success or failure in the crucible of competition."

Maiden's traditional Scottish approach tended to discourage the so-called fancy shots. "Except in most unusual positions," Kiltie told Keeler one day, "the best way to play any golf club is to play it the way it was designed to be played." Keeler described Kiltie's style:

JONES'S BREAKTHROUGH IN MAJOR CHAMPIONSHIP GOLF CAME IN 1923 WHEN HE WON THE U.S. OPEN CONTESTED AT THE INWOOD COUNTRY CLUB IN LONG ISLAND, NEW YORK.

Stewart Maiden, never going out for tournaments but a magnificently sound and orthodox player in the old days at East Lake, was accustomed to bang his full mashie shots up there from a crisp, clean impact, the club's face taking the ball with its normal loft and the blade merely shearing the grass in front of the ball's erstwhile position, instead of hacking out a divot six inches long. And as I recall it, the ball used to behave pretty well on reaching the greens—which were not watered in the good old days at East Lake.

Kiltie's golfing philosophy was employed as the bedrock of Jones's own theories of golf. For instance, Jones's strategy of stroking putts to "die" at the hole was borrowed from Kiltie. "When the ball dies at the hole," said Stewart, "there are four doors; the ball can go in at the front, or the back, or at either side, wherever it touches the rim. But a ball that comes up to the hole with speed on it must hit the front door fairly in the middle; there are no side doors, and no Sunday entrance, for the putt that arrives under speed."

As with all Scottish players, Kiltie was efficient but also a very fast player. Jones developed into a fast player as well. Former USGA Executive Director Joe Dey watched Jones play his amateur championship matches in 1930 at Merion. "My notes show that it took only 2 hours 10 minutes for the 14 holes of Jones's first round match at Merion against C. Ross (Sandy) Somerville of Canada. That's an average of 9.3 minutes per hole or about 2 hours 48 minutes for 18 holes," said Dey. Most golf strokes are but repetitions of countless hundreds played before. Only a few situations require considerable study before deciding the best remedy. Both Kiltie and Jones agreed that taking too long in the execution of a golf stroke tended to promote the one most unwanted thing of all—tension.

"Whenever I see a much-considered shot go astray, I can't help thinking of the lawyer who had unsuccessfully defended a client charged with murder," Jones used to say. "The trial had been long drawn out, lasting nearly a month, and the lawyer had made quite a lot of noise and stormed eloquently in his argument. Meeting a brother lawyer on the street a few days later, the case came up in discussion, and the lawyer asked his friend what he thought of his conduct of the trial. His friend replied, "Well, I think you could have reached the same result with a whole lot less effort."

Jones believed that a player should form the habit of playing promptly with freedom and rhythm so as to avoid the opportunity for tension to set up.

I used to be a very rapid player. I am still fairly fast—after I've taken my stance. But at Merion in 1925 I discovered that I was missing a lot of shots simply because I was hitting the ball too soon after I had reached it, especially on the putting green. Having walked up to the green at a brisk pace, and elbowed my way through whatever gallery there might have been, I had been putting quickly while my breath was coming in short gasps and my ears ringing as I leaned over the ball. Realizing that I was making a mistake, I resolved that no matter how much time I had consumed, I was going to tranquilize my breathing before I made another putt . . . but after taking the stance it is too late to worry. The only thing to do then is hit the ball!

Kiltie's Protégés

In 1925 Bob and protégé Watts Gunn were the only two members of the same club ever to play in the finals of a major championship—the Amateur Championship at Oakmont. Back home in Atlanta, Stewart read about Jones's wild drives off the tee that were catching the ferocious furrowed bunkers of Oakmont. Maiden sent Jones a telegram "Hit it hard. It'll land somewhere." Jones did as he was told, and while it did not straighten out his drives, he was able to hit over the bunkers and at least have a reasonable approach to the greens. It made all the difference in the world in carrying away the Havemeyer Trophy to East Lake.

THE ONLY OCCASION UPON WHICH TWO MEMBERS OF THE SAME
GOLF CLUB HAVE MET IN THE FINALS OF A MAJOR
CHAMPIONSHIP WAS IN 1925 WHEN WATTS GUNN MET BOB
JONES FOR THE FINALS OF THE U.S. AMATEUR CHAMPIONSHIP
CONTESTED AT OAKMONT COUNTRY CLUB. WATTS ASKED
BOB JONES, "BOB, ARE YOU GOING TO GIVE ME MY USUAL TWO
STROKES ASIDE LIKE YOU DO AT EAST LAKE?" BOB SHOT BACK,
"I'M GOING TO GIVE YOU HELL YOU LITTLE S.O.B." JONES
PREVAILED 8 AND 7.

Stewart was with Jones in 1927 when he successfully defended his British Open title at St. Andrews. In
the early rounds Jones couldn't buy a putt. Kiltie then
remarked that if Bob ever got to missing his big shots,
he might sink some putts. In the third round, Jones did
just that while returning a score of 68 which was a record

THE "SOUTHERN HURRICANE" WATTS
GUNN HOLDS THE RECORD OF WINNING 15
STRAIGHT HOLES AGAINST VINCENT
BRADFORD IN THE 1925 U.S. AMATEUR AT
OAKMONT.

in competition at the Old Course. That night Kiltie pre-
dicted to O.B. Keeler that Jones would win, "No man
can beat him when he's hitting the ball like this." In
the final round, Jones needed 34 putts in his round of
72, but Kiltie was immutable. As Darwin might say,
Maiden possessed a charm of silent loyalty belonging
to an age that is now almost gone. Before Bob had even
finished, Stewart poked Colonel Jones, Bob's father, in
the ribs, "Let's go. It's all over." The Colonel quizzically

asked, "What's all over?" "The show. He's in," said Kiltie curtly. Just by watching Bob's silky swing, Maiden knew the result before the finish.

In 1926 Jones conceived the secret idea of winning all the major championships on both sides of the Atlantic Ocean—The Grand Slam. Although Jones told no one, not even his friend and biographer O.B. Keeler, Stewart Maiden must have guessed. The man of few words didn't have to be told what he could see with his own eyes. Jones was the greatest, and no one would stop him. Although Bob won half of the Grand Slam in 1926—the British and American Opens—he had a few other venues to travel before administering the coup de grace. Nor would they stop, the other famous pupils of Kiltie's—Watts Gunn, Charlie Yates, and Louise Suggs. Known as the "Southern Hurricane," Watts Gunn once took 15 holes in a row from Vincent Bradford in the 1925 Amateur at Oakmont. When asked how he did it, Watts could only say, "All I know is I'm tired and hungry. I'm so hungry my pants are about to fall off!" Watts faced Jones in the finals of that championship. Who knows how Kiltie divided his loyalties between these two students. Before the match, Watts asked Bob, "Are you going to give me my usual two strokes a side?" Bob shot back, "I'm going to give you hell, you little s.o.b." And he promptly proceeded to do so, defeating Watts 8 and 7. Watts won the U.S. Intercollegiate in 1927 and both the Southern Amateur and Southern Open in 1928.

Charmin' Charlie Yates's family lived on Second Avenue across from East Lake Golf Club. Charlie was 16 years old when Bob Jones won the Grand Slam, so he was within the watchful eye of Kiltie. Charlie added the seventeenth major East Lake championship when he won the 1938 British Amateur. Charlie also won the 1934 U.S. Intercollegiate and 1935 Western Amateur.

THE EAST LAKE GOLF CLUB BEFORE THE NOVEMBER 23, 1925 FIRE
THAT ENGULFED THE CLUBHOUSE. NOTE THE TIMBERS EVIDENCED IN
THE TUDOR VERSION OF THE CLUBHOUSE. THE TIMBERS WERE REMOVED
AND NOT REPLACED DURING THE REBUILDING OF THE CLUBHOUSE FOR
INSURANCE PURPOSES.

CHARLIE YATES IS PRESENTED THE 1938 BRITISH AMATEUR CHAMPI-
ONSHIP CUP BY ROYAL TROON CAPTAIN W. LINDSAY CARLOW.

WATTS GUNN RETAINED HIS AMATEUR STATUS
THROUGHOUT HIS LIFETIME.

As late as 1941 Kiltie appeared on the front page of
the *Atlanta Journal* looking over the golf swing of Louise
Suggs, a Lithia Springs star. Just by watching Louise
swing the club, Maiden suggested "her trouble usually
started about 50 yards from the flag." He saw her position at the top was flawed and Louise sheepishly admitted he was perfectly right. She learned her lesson
well, winning 50 championships in a long career.

Maiden took several "breaks" from his East Lake
post in the early years. In 1913 he accompanied George
Adair on a trip to England and Scotland to study golf

STEWART MAIDEN WITH HIS FAMOUS PUPIL BOBBY JONES AT THE 1921 NATIONAL AMATEUR CHAMPIONSHIP CONTESTED AT ST. LOUIS.

course architecture. Stewart also barely missed qualifying in the British Open Championship held at Hoylake, scoring 82 and 79 in the qualifying rounds and missing the cut by two strokes. Upon return to Atlanta, Donald Ross was engaged to redesign the old Bendelow course with their ideas.

In September 1913 Kiltie hosted some special guests at East Lake. That was the year Harry Vardon and Ted Ray were vanquished at Brookline by Francis Ouimet in the Open. Vardon and Ray then traveled south to play an exhibition against Kiltie and Willie Mann. Ray was forced to make a seven-foot birdie putt on the last green to win 1 up. It was Little Bob Jones's first glimpse at big-time golfers. The small fledgling golfer must have been astonished to see Ray strike the ball with such force that divots as big as footprints flew in the wake of his strokes.

In the spring of 1919 Stewart left East Lake for a brief post at the St. Louis Country Club. Maiden became acquainted with many of the members there and taught member Audrey Faust who later won the Missouri State Women's Championship. The following year he returned to East Lake but promised that he would come back to St. Louis if a major championship was secured. So the St. Louis Country Club petitioned the USGA in November 1920 for permission to host the National Amateur Championship. Approval was then granted to St. Louis to host the first Amateur held west of the Mississippi River in September 1921. Bob Jones played but was still in the summer of his seven lean years and lost to Willie Hunter in the third round when he tried to cut the dogleg and drive the green on the eighth hole but hit the top twig of the tallest tree. The "Boston Seige Gun" Jesse Guilford won that title against Bob Gardner in the finals.

Kiltie & Keeler

In 1927 Keeler rejoiced with Bobby Jones in the homeland of Kiltie during a homecoming to Carnoustie on the heels of Bob's successful defense of his Open title at St. Andrews. Visiting Kiltie's hometown was the least Jones could do for the genius who showed Jones the key to his success. Keeler noted his astonishment at the event:

> In all my experience in golf, which has been certainly
> not brief and perhaps not inconsiderable, there is noth-
> ing that quite compares with that pilgrimage to
> Carnoustie across the Tay River from St. Andrews. Even
> Stewart, the taciturn Caledonian, loosened up.

How proud Kiltie must have been when a thousand
Scotsmen met the ferry boat and heard the piper greet
the Jones party. And how astonished Jones must have
been when 6,000 townspeople crowded together to see
him golf on the links the following day. Keeler's journal
recorded the scene when Kiltie's friends he'd not seen
in 20 years greeted him nonchalantly as if it had been
20 minutes.

And where was Kiltie on the other occasions when
the great Bob Jones did his magic and exorcised the
demons and carried away the silver? After all, the Silent Scot was there when Jones narrowly lost the Open
to Sarazen at Skokie in 1922. And he was also sitting in
the corner of the room at the Grand Hotel after Jones
posted the record low round of 68 during the 1927 British Open. Yes, Kiltie was "there" for Jones at crucial
times in his life. And as the story of their lives unfolded,
Bob Jones would not forget his good friend either.

If ever there was a reporter qualified to conduct a
proper interview with someone like Stewart Maiden
surely O.B. Keeler would be on top of the list. After all,
Keeler was the first reporter ever to get a complete interview with Bobby Jones in 1926. And Keeler got the
first interview with the Prince of Wales on golf in 1930.
Keeler also was the first to broadcast a British Open
Championship live across the ocean to America. So
surely Keeler could get the essence of Kiltie in a story,
couldn't he?

Well, Keeler took several shots at the task. In 1915
Pop was assigned to get a Sunday story from Kiltie be-

fore the Southern Amateur was to be played at East Lake. The old thing, you know, about the tournament and the players and their chances for success. Keeler recalled the interview:

> Well, I got a column. A whole column. But I wasn't precisely set up about it. It was on the hypothetical question order as exploited in our courts of law. In the entire column, Stewart Maiden was quoted three times. He said "yes" once and "no" twice.

In 1922 Keeler interviewed Kiltie on "the most common faults" in the golf swing. As Keeler noted, "Maiden is one of the most consistently and thoroughly reticent Scots your correspondent has ever encountered." During the interview Keeler learned that one common fault was "trying to think after the stroke is started." Kiltie then made a "singularly fine explanation of that broad term concentration." "Do your thinking before you start the swing. You won't be likely to do it afterward." Keeler's interpretation was "to think of nothing but the shot" while making the stroke.

From this exercise, Pop Keeler learned that the proper answer to the question "What is the commonest fault in golf" is distilled into the phrase "Hitting too soon."

Surely Kiltie noticed Young Jones was "hitting too soon" in the early part of his career after he was entrenched in the habit of throwing away his clubs after a terrible shot. As Jones's caddy, Luke Ross, recounted:

> After he'd throw a club I'd run and get it and rush right back to him. He'd usually follow quickly with another poor shot.
>
> One day Stewart Maiden, Bobby's pro at East Lake in Atlanta, and I talked about how we might get him to

overcome this problem. We decided that whenever he'd throw a club, I should walk slowly back and give him time to cool off. It seemed to work.

That's not to say Keeler never got anything out of Kiltie at all. Quite the contrary. Kiltie gave Keeler that splendid interview on golf psychology titled "Shoot the Works" published in the *American Golfer* in December 27, 1924. Even though Keeler couldn't break 90 on the course, he never took a formal lesson from Kiltie. Instead, Pop challenged him with his evocative "cross-examination" style of interview in an effort to learn his secrets. Trying to entice Kiltie to step out on a limb with an opinion about what he might do in a particular situation, Pop set the stage: "If I had been playing Willie Hunter in a National Championship and was 2 up and 8 to go, I think I would not have tried to cut off the dogleg on the eighth hole at St. Louis." Kiltie looked at Pop and didn't skip a beat with his reply: "Don't lose any sleep over what you would do playing Willie Hunter in a championship!" To Kiltie, like Bob Jones, there was golf and then there was championship golf. The two are not remotely the same.

Golf Club Craftsman

As the head East Lake professional, Kiltie was also probably underrated as a fine craftsman of golf clubs. East Lake member Arch Martin recalled:

> It was so interesting to watch him fashion a golf club—
> either fashion a head of a driver and put the shaft in it
> or take an iron head and put a shaft in it. There was an
> art in it, and he knew it from the beginning. He used to
> take a rough hickory shaft and fashion that thing and

shape it, reduce the size of it to give it a little "whip" as they called it. And he would use varnish and cottonseed oil and some ink black to bark the grain in the wood. Then he would polish it down to a very fine finish and then put on a leather grip and strips, twisting it around and around to end the thing, then securing it at the end with a tack and some linen thread . . . he kept a supply of ready-made clubs and people were continually breaking shafts, particularly our Bob Jones.

Bobby's first clubs included the cut-down cleek given to him by Fulton Coleville and a putter and one of his mother's cut-down brassies. In the Christmas of 1909, Colonel Bob Jones decided that his son ought to have some better clubs and got Stewart Maiden to make up a complete set. He was also accorded permission by the green committee at East Lake to use the course except on Saturdays and Sundays. There's no telling how many sets of Stewart Maiden clubs were devoured in the first East Lake fire of 1914. Clearly Bob Jones's clubs and those of O.B. Keeler went up in smoke. They were, of course, replaced and went up in smoke a second time during the 1925 East Lake fire. That is, all but Bob Jones's Calamity Jane putter, which must have been under Jones's bed and not in the club room at East Lake with the rest of his clubs. Beginning in 1926 Jones assembled his Grand Slam set of golf clubs, which included several made by Stewart Maiden and carried his name. Jones's favorite spoon with "Stewart Maiden" and a yellow stripe across the crown of the clubhead still reposes in the trophy room of Augusta National Golf Club.

Through the late 1920s, Old Tom Stewart of St. Andrews shipped forged iron heads to Maiden, who finished them for his club members. In June 1929 the Wilson Golf Company celebrated Kiltie in a full-page tribute published in *Golf Illustrated* entitled "Bobby Jones Calls

JAMES MAIDEN AT THE NASSAU COUNTRY CLUB, CIRCA 1923
A FEW YEARS AFTER HE GIFTED CALAMITY JANE I PUTTER
TO BOB JONES.

Him 'The First Doctor of Golf.' " The text of the tribute included the following:

> Far to the front in the game's Hall of Fame belongs the name of Stewart Maiden. On the cobbles of the little sea-level village of Carnoustie, in Scotland, as a barefoot boy in wee kilties, he battered homemade cork balls with improvised sticks, and acquired the name "Kiltie," which has adhered to him ever since. For companions he had half a dozen other boys who have since also become famous, some of them champions in America. . . .

Following the Grand Slam in 1930, both Jones and Kiltie understood that life was not going to be the same. "It's great that the boy now has won all the major titles there are," Kiltie said, "but it's sad in a way too, for there's nothing left for him to win. All the rest of his victories will be just repetitions." Kiltie "retired" from East Lake and traveled to New York where he operated an exclusive indoor golf studio in the "New York Central Building" across the street from Grand Central Station. The "Stewart Maiden Golf School" was located at 225 Park Avenue (phone Murray Hill 2-0156). It was listed in the New York phone book from 1935 to 1938. He signed on with the Hillerich & Bradsby Company of Louisville, Kentucky, to design his own brand of clubs. The "Grand Slam golf clubs designed by Stewart Maiden" became very popular. Maiden incorporated a compact blade design with a distinctive flange sole not unlike the one pioneered by Bob Jones himself with the Spalding Company. The irons carried a "B-bow" hickory shaft and also Tru-temper "compensator" steel shafts. The Stewart Maiden "Model 20" wooden clubs were "balanced in such a way as to give a golfer the sensation of throwing the clubhead through the ball." Maiden also developed a club-fitting chart designed to custom fit clubs based upon a player's physical type and his reach measured by length of his arms. This innovative technique is still used in today's "modern" club-fitting "systems."

Maiden was impressed with the quality control of the H&B organization.

When I was asked to design a set of clubs that would be correct for 90 percent of golfers, I hesitated because I had had experience in selecting golf clubs for my pupils and knew how difficult it was to get a set of golf clubs

Jones finally won the British Amateur Championship in 1930 at St. Andrews. The Captain of the Royal and Ancient Golf Club Colonel Skene presents the venerable trophy to the champion during the first leg of the Grand Slam.

matched in all particulars. I knew the years that some of my pupils had spent picking up here and there clubs that were of first one make and then another, that were not matched as far as appearance is concerned, but were matched in the essential factors that go to make up a perfect matched set. I doubted the ability of any organization to turn out clubs according to my ideals.

I think those who know me know that I would not lend my name to any enterprise that I did not believe in thoroughly. I actually designed the clubs that bear my name. Designed them out of my rich experience of years in teaching golf and fitting players with golf clubs. You can buy lots of clubs more dolled up than these are, and for less money, but I don't believe you will find anywhere sets of clubs that are more correct from the play ability angle, or whose lines promote so effectively the confidence that is so essential to good golf.

Interestingly, Maiden deliberately designed his clubs to have "flat" lies rather than an upright style. He believed that a flat lie promoted a golfer addressing the ball with a straight left arm in a more natural way than having to "arch" the wrist up to achieve a proper address. Also because most golfers tended to slice the ball, Kiltie designed the blades to have deep faces to counteract the slice.

Being from New York himself, Grantland Rice did all he could to help Stewart Maiden get established in New York. The price of a lesson was steep—about $20 an hour—but it seemed that everyone wanted to learn from "Bobby Jones's Doctor." Business was brisk. Kiltie also spent time playing and teaching at Sands Point Golf Club in Port Washington, New York.

The Lost Lessons

By 1923 Kiltie's golfing students, Alexa Stirling, Bobby Jones, and Perry Adair, had already collected 13 golf titles. By that time nearly everyone wanted to know the secret method of the Silent Scot. Pop Keeler continually tried to get Kiltie to share his secrets. Finally in 1923, Kiltie agreed to write a series of articles for the *Outdoor South* magazine of which Keeler was editor-in-chief. These collected writings were published in a

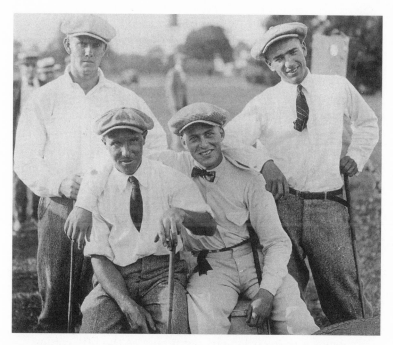

HARRISON JOHNSTON, KILTIE MAIDEN, BOB JONES, AND LEO DEIGEL *(LEFT TO RIGHT)* AT INVERNESS COUNTRY CLUB, TOLEDO, OHIO, IN 1920.

small booklet titled "Stewart Maiden's Ten Lessons in Golf." Maiden expounded his theories on the grip, stance, putting, chip shot, medium and full pitch, iron and wood club play, hip action, and timing. These ideas were supplemented by Keeler's articles published in the *American Golfer* on "The Most Common Faults" (1922) and "Shoot the Works" (1924). In June 1930 Maiden also published an *American Golfer* article titled "Sound Fundamentals" in which he explained the basics that were imparted to Alexa Stirling and Bobby Jones early in their golfing lives. After Maiden joined Hillerich & Bradsby as a consultant in 1932, Maiden wrote the "Three Essentials of Better Golf," describing the right grip, balance, and clubs. Kiltie also expanded on a dozen total subjects including tips on the tee shot, the approach shots, backspin, the short game, bunker shots, putting, the left side, and use of the number 9 iron. There was a limited distribution of the "Three Essentials of Better Golf" primarily to the customers and professionals who used H&B products. Both these writings and the "Ten Lessons in Golf" have been completely forgotten by the golfing public since they were published. Years later even Pop Keeler completely forgot about Kiltie's writings. In January 1941 Kiltie traveled from New York to spend the holidays with his Atlanta friend Jack Bothamley. In an article entitled, "Stewart Maiden Here—Recalls Jones' Triumphs," Keeler wrote:

> Kiltie the Kingmaker—the silent Scot; the least talkative golfing professional that ever came out of Carnoustie or any other part of Scotland; who never wrote any books of instruction; who never went in the movies and regarded photographers as the fifth columnists along with death, war, pestilence, and famine; Stewart Maiden who came to the East Lake Country Club in 1908 to find there among others Perry Adair and Alexa Stirling and Bobby Jones; who now administers golf instruction to a select coterie of pupils and disciples at his studio in the Grand Central Building New York and at long last came back to Atlanta for a little visit with his old friends.

If Pop Keeler, who arranged with Kiltie to write his instruction book in the first place, forgot about Kiltie's golf writings, then it is safe to say everyone else did too. It is equally safe to say that, once reminded, Pop would enthusiastically underscore the importance of what Kiltie thought about the fundamentals of golf and their importance in golf literature history.

Kiltie's Family

Kiltie and his wife Annie Rogers had two daughters, Roger Mae and Frances. The pressures of living with a genius like Kiltie must have been considerable. Whatever the cause, Kiltie's marriage dissolved in the late 1930s. Thereafter he seemed to struggle with depression. Kiltie was not in the infrequent company of his pint. Sometimes he reminisced about meeting New York Mayor Jimmy Walker during Jones's 1930 ticker-tape parade and together getting pie-eyed at a fashionable New York hotel that evening. Other times Kiltie simply treated his melancholy condition with strong beverages over extended periods of time. His old friend Bob Jones always kept a close eye on him. Whenever Jones felt that Kiltie needed a rest from his circumstances, he would call brother Jimmy Maiden in New York. Jimmy's son, "Cam" Maiden, recalled those times when Uncle Stewart came to visit. "There's no doubt he was extremely quiet," said Cam. "He was an avid reader and could bury himself in a book for hours and you wouldn't hear a peep out of him." Kiltie took a special liking to Cam. Kiltie often went with Cam to some of the vacant fairways of Nassau Country Club and watched him hit practice balls. "Then one day he met a very attractive socialite named Ms. Rose. They got along tremendously, and Uncle Stewart was very happy. He was really animated in her presence and didn't seem depressed at all. They had a great time together," Cam remembered. Kiltie did occasionally visit his daughters who settled in Washington, D.C. When daughter Roger Mae was pregnant with his grandson, Kiltie pointed with great pride and announced, "You've got Kiltie in there." In fact, Maiden's namesake grandson is today known as Kiltie.

Homecoming

In 1947 Bob Jones and some friends bought some plantation property in Atlanta and retained architect Robert Trent Jones to build the Peachtree Golf Club. Construction of the course extended into the next year. Jones thought it would be a good idea if his old friend Kiltie was invested as the first golf professional.

One of the first lessons Kiltie gave when he returned to Atlanta was to Bobby Jones's own son, Bob Jones III. Bob III became an enthusiastic golfer, qualified for several U.S. Amateur Championships, and even once won the Atlanta City Championship. His father, however, wanted to make sure that he played only for fun and never for money. The elder Jones conceived a plan to discourage his son from aspiring to the professional ranks. A lesson for Bob III was arranged with Kiltie. The student promptly arrived at East Lake at the top of the morning and began launching hundreds of practice balls under Kiltie's watchful eye. At noon the young man put his club down and started walking toward the East Lake Clubhouse. "Laddie, where do you think you're going?" asked Kiltie. "To have lunch," replied Bob III. "Come back here—I don't take lunch," announced Kiltie. Bob III got the message loud and clear and became a businessman, much to his father's relief.

Kiltie's homecoming to Atlanta after two decades was front-page sports news. He lived in the plantation house converted into Peachtree's new clubhouse. However, Kiltie never got to enjoy his new position. In October 1948 he suffered a stroke that rendered him paralyzed and unconscious. On the same floor of his hospital, Bob Jones was recovering from an operation to remove bony spurs from his neck. Jones's doctors knew of the exceptionally close relationship that bound these great men

BOB JONES DISCUSSES THE NEW PEACHTREE GOLF CLUB WITH ITS FIRST PROFESSIONAL, STEWART MAIDEN, IN 1948. THIS WAS TAKEN ONLY A FEW MONTHS BEFORE MAIDEN PASSED AWAY.

THE SAMUEL HOUSE PLANTATION SERVED AS THE HEADQUARTERS OF GENERAL GEORGE SHERMAN DURING HIS CIVIL WAR MARCH TO THE SEA IN 1865. IT WAS THEREFORE SPARED DESTRUCTION. IN 1948, THE PLANTATION HOUSE BECAME THE PEACHTREE GOLF CLUB CLUBHOUSE WHERE STEWART MAIDEN SERVED AS THE FIRST GOLF PROFESSIONAL IN 1948.

together. They knew that Bob and Kiltie had plumbed the depths of golfing despair together and had climbed the mountaintop of greatness, too. Together Bob and Kiltie had stood on the ultimate craig of golf's Mt. Olympus and looked out upon the vistas that no other men had seen. Together they had sacrificed with each other and for each other. And together they lay in the same hospital in grave circumstances. Perhaps for these reasons, Jones's doctors could not bring themselves to tell Jones about his dear friend's afflictions several doors away. The news may well have caused hearts to break and piled one tragedy upon another.

Kiltie's game of life was called for darkness when he passed away on November 4, 1948. He was 62. Bob Jones was not told of his dear friend's demise until three days later. His grief was no less devastating than if the news was more timely. Front-page eulogies to the Kingmaker extended from the *Atlanta Journal* to the *New York Times*.

Bobby Jones's "Boswell," O.B. Keeler, wrote in the *Journal* what was in the hearts of his friends:

> Some way, you never seem to expect a time when Stewart Maiden wouldn't be around—anyway if you're concerned with golf in any form . . . Somewhere, and you hope nearby, Kiltie the Kingmaker always would be around . . . No. I don't think Stewart Maiden's gone away. And it's not only that his record in the great game is entrenched with that of his disciple, "safely and forever within the Impregnable Quadrilateral of Golf."
>
> No. In a greater game, which we call Life, Stewart Maiden will always be around and deeply enclosed in the hearts of those who know and love him.
>
> Seldom in the history of sports have so many owed so much to a man of so few words.

TEN LESSONS IN GOLF

STEWART MAIDEN

General Suggestions

Golfers take up the game in a variety of ways, but I suppose the majority of them in this country simply start playing, as they took up baseball. Some of them start as children and of course they have the best chance. A great many do not get started until they are grown, and they have far more difficulty in becoming proficient, especially as most of them, in picking up the game and acquiring some sort of method, usually pick up and ac-quire a number of wrong ideas and habits, which have to be corrected if they are to play a proper game. Con-trary to a widespread supposition, Bob Jones did not begin learning golf by his father bringing him to me to teach him. He started out before he was six years old, with a sawed-off cleek, on a five-hole course laid out by himself about the yard of his home near the East Lake Club, with one hole, I think, out in the street. That is as good a way to start as any, I think. Less than a year later his parents moved into a cottage in the East Lake Club property and Bob began watching me play and imitating my style, as any child will do if he has the chance to see anyone play a game that he himself wants to play, and believes that person to be good at it. For a number of years his style was almost identical with mine. It has changed a good deal in the last 10 years, but he told me not long ago he could go out and swing and hit a ball just as I do today. Basically, I suppose, his method still is founded on mine, and he has done pretty well with it. I taught Miss Alexa Stirling almost from the beginning of her study of golf, and she, too, has done very well. Perhaps this indicates that my method is sound.

THE SWING

Before starting to read the following lessons, which are designed for beginners and for players who started the game without adequate instruction and wish to improve their play, I wish to say a few things in a general way.

There are three main kinds of swing in golf—flat, upright, and medium. Which is best for a player depends on his build and his inclination. A short, stout man almost always uses, and should use, a flat swing; that is, a swing in which the club, if carried as far as possible in the backswing, would strike him back of the shoulders. The upright swing usually suits tall and slender players, and with it the backswing if carried to excess would strike about the back of the neck. The medium, naturally, is between the others; and for normally constructed players I think it is best. Indeed, I like the medium swing for all golfers, within the aforementioned limitations of anatomy. My advice in all swings is that even for the longest shots the club not be carried back so far that the club dips below the horizontal. This advice is stressed in the case of stout players or those past the resiliency of youth. It is a rule almost invariably disregarded by women players, who usually overswing badly and add thereby another difficulty to a game already difficult enough.

The Left Arm

Another prime fault of a great many golfers is a tendency to bend the left arm as the top of the swing is approached in taking the club back for the shot. I would set it out as an inflexible rule that the left arm should be kept straight all the way to the top of the backswing, and maintained straight and even rigid all the way through the downward swing, until after the ball has been hit. This will help in several ways, one of them being to keep the player automatically from over-swinging. Also, it forces the player, in order to get the club back freely, to bend both wrists under the shaft, instead of bending or "breaking" the left wrist the wrong way— namely, in the direction faced by the palm instead of bending it away from the palm; a glance at the pictures accompanying the first lesson will show the correct method.

Wrist Action

Wrist action is supremely important in the golf stroke, and good play cannot possibly be attained without proper use of the wrists. If the hands are settled on the club in either of the grips described in the first lesson, and the club then is turned away from the ball as it is taken back, and the left arm is kept straight, it practically compels the player to bend his wrists properly, and "set" them for discharging the power of the shot. It is my aim to make this wrist action as nearly automatic as possible, and this really can be done if the student will grip the club properly, keep the left arm straight in the backswing, and turn the hands under the club as it goes to the top of the stroke. At that point of a full stroke both hands should be exactly under the shaft and both wrists well bent or "set."

THE CLUBS

One of the best ways to learn to play golf is to start out with a single club, preferably a midiron—the No. 2 iron of the series—but nearly every beginner wants more of an outfit, and for his first selection I would suggest for wood clubs a brassie and a spoon; and for the others a No. 2 iron, a deep mashie, a niblick, and a putter. Others will inevitably be acquired, and pretty rapidly. As to a guide in the choice of the original set, I cannot be of much help. As a rule, a club is good for you if you feel as if you could hit the ball with it. There are plenty of good standard lines on the market, and if you like the feel of a club, you may as well try it. The usual length for men's clubs is 36 to 38 inches for the irons and pitching clubs, and 41 to 43 inches for the woods. Women's clubs are lighter and a couple of inches shorter, usually. The measurement is from the heel of the head to the end of the shaft. In the matter of putters, help yourself. There are hundreds of kinds, and you will be changing all the time anyway, so you may freely indulge any fancy that may strike you. I think thin grips are best; that is, a grip with little or no padding under the leather. But that also is a matter of personal preference.

THE BALL

You will do well, if a beginner, to get a large-size, tough-covered ball to start with. The standard-size, heavy, high-tension ball is fine for the expert, but is not suited to beginners and duffers. Also, it is easier to cut, and it does not get up so well from any club, or respond so readily to a light or inaccurate stroke. However, if you have a mind to use the same ball that the experts use, go ahead. Experience is a great teacher in everything, especially in golf.

Lesson I—The Grip

The first thing to be considered in playing a proper golf shot of any kind is the grip—that is, the way a player takes hold of the club. In teaching golf I have noticed that almost every beginner naturally takes hold of the club in a wrong way, from which I conclude there is no such thing as a natural grip in golf; that is, a correct natural grip. It is possible to play very bad golf with a correct grip, but is practically impossible to play good golf with an incorrect grip, so that is where we shall start in these lessons—at a correct grip. There is more than one correct grip, in golf, and I do not try to teach every pupil the same one. Personally, I prefer the Vardon or overlapping grip and teach it to all pupils who like it and have the hands to use it. That, and the plain old-fashioned "Two-Vs" grip are the leading methods today, and in my opinion one or the other will be suited to anybody who wants to play golf.

In both grips the club is held in the fingers, not in the palms. At one time, playing the old gutta-percha ball, the palm grip, with the club held firmly in both fists, was prevalent. It is out-of-date today, though a few very fine players employ it for full shots.

In either the "Two-Vs" or the Vardon grip, the left hand lays hold of the club in the same manner, the shaft resting in the fingers, with the hand sufficiently on top of the club so you can see the first two knuckles as the club is placed back of the ball, ready to play. In the "Two-Vs" grip the right hand then is applied to the club so

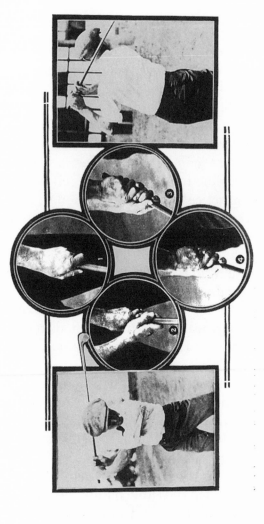

The Grip. No. 1 shows the application of the left hand to the club for all shots except the putt. No. 2 is the regular Vardon grip for the full shot, of which No. 3 is the side view. No. 4 is the side view of the grip for putting, showing two fingers of the right hand overlapping instead of one. This is not at all necessary—it is an individual development. At the left is shown the correct position of the hands at the top of the swing. At the right, the finish. Note that the right hand appears to hold loosely and the left firmly.

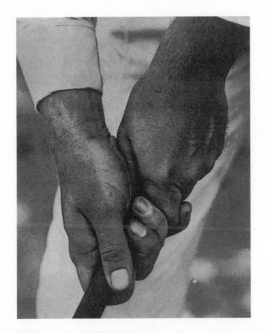

Bobby Jones shows the grip he uses for the drive.

that the shaft also rests in the fingers, the inverted angle made by the thumb and forefinger pointing in practically the same direction as that made by the same angle of the left thumb and forefinger—like two "Vs" aiming almost toward the left shoulder as the ball is addressed; that is where the grip gets its name.

The hands are brought snugly together; there must never be any space between them; and from this circumstance, I suppose, grew the Vardon method, which brings the hands yet closer together by overlapping the little finger of the right hand on the forefinger of the left, encouraging the two hands to work as a unit, with not much chance of any opposition, which is ruinous to the stroke.

If you have large and strong hands, I advise the

Vardon grip. If your hands are small or not strong, you probably will do better with the older style, which is used by Chick Evans, who has short fingers, and certainly has served him well. Cyril Tolley, the longest hitter in the world, perhaps, also uses the plain grip. Bob Jones uses the overlapping grip, and most of the first-rank golfers of the day do also. Jock Hutchinson goes so far as to overlap two fingers even in his full shots but I do not advise this for anyone who has not enormous hands, as Jock has.

Either of the grips described will answer for every shot except putting, in which the hands should be less on top of the shaft; the palms facing each other so that the wrists "break" opposite each other and in one line. In other shots the "heel" of the left hand is more toward the objective of the shot, giving more power and snap in the stroke.

In putting, a good many golfers—I am one of them—overlap with two fingers, while others put all the right hand on the shaft and overlap its little finger with the forefinger of the left. Bob Jones uses the latter method. But putting, as you will discover, is a game within a game and has a style pretty much all its own.

The grip has much effect on the stroke. If a player is pulling his shots he frequently can correct the tendency by turning his left hand slightly toward the left on the club and putting the right hand more on top of the shaft. If slicing, the left hand should be more on top of the club, and the right hand farther under it—that is, turned so that the back is pointing more toward the ground.

As a general rule for full shots, the left hand holds firmly and the right rather loosely during the swing until just before impact, when the right will tighten instinctively. A golf stroke is a delicate matter, much the same as a billiard stroke, despite the power applied in the full shots, and the grip should favor delicacy and the factor known as "touch." This means a finger-grip and a comfortable, smooth-working method that permits the club a free swing down the line of the shot.

MAY 1931 ADVERTISEMENT.

Lesson II—The Stance

After taking hold of the golf club the next thing a player does is to stand up to the ball, and his manner of doing this is called the stance. There are three kinds of stance, known as square, open, and closed. In the square stance, the player's feet are level—that is, the toes are on a line exactly parallel with the line of the shot. In the open stance the left foot is farther from the line of the shot, so that the player is partly facing the objective to which he is playing. In the closed, the right foot is far- ther from the line. In the old days, the square stance was popular. After the lively ball was introduced, a gen- eral change of method took place and the open stance became more popular, and latterly there has been some- thing of a return toward the square stance. The closed stance is not usual, though some fine players employ it, and it is possible, I think, to get a harder swing from it, since the position of the feet favors a free pivot in the backswing. George Duncan, one of the greatest of the modern British professionals, some years ago adopted a slightly closed stance in driving to correct a tendency to slice. Harrison Johnston, a crack American amateur, uses a very closed stance in nearly all shots, for the same reason.

I like a nearly square stance, very slightly opened, for full shots, opening the stance as the iron clubs come into play, and taking a quite open position for short pitches and chip shots. This is about Bob Jones's method, also, though Bob's feet are closer together in all shots

THE STANCE. No. 1 IS THE POSITION OF THE FEET IN THE STANCE FOR A FULL
WOOD SHOT, No. 2, WITH THE CLUB AT THE TOP OF THE SWING, AND No. 3, AT
THE FINISH. No. 4 IS THE ADDRESS FOR AN IRON SHOT, AND No. 5 AT THE TOP
OF THE SWING. NOTE THAT THE LEFT HEEL BARELY LEAVES THE TURF AT THE
TOP OF THE SWING. No. 6 IS THE STANCE FOR THE PUTT.

BOBBY JONES DEMONSTRATING THE
FINISH OF THE DRIVE.

than those of any first-class player I can call to mind.
He is said to have the "narrowest" stance of any great
player. In short pitches and chip shots his heels are practically together.

In the normal full shot, the ball customarily is played
about opposite the left heel, perhaps a trifle inside it.
The position of the ball with regard to the feet naturally has a great effect on the stroke, and some golfers
have a style that places the ball midway between the
feet, and others nearer the line of the right foot, but in
my opinion both these methods and especially the last
are the result of some peculiarity in the swing and are

not recommended for orthodox study. The idea, of course, is to place the ball so that the club will encounter it at the very bottom of the swing; and the orthodox swing should constitute that point about opposite the left shoulder. If you will stand up for a full shot and sole the club back of the ball, the left shoulder, left arm, and the club will be nearly in line, and that is the position, approximately, for the club to take hold of the ball in the stroke.

As the grip influences the stroke greatly, so does the stance. Other things being normal, the closed stance favors a pull, the club coming on the ball from inside the line of the shot, and the open stance favors a slice, as the club naturally inclines to come on the ball from outside the line. I would advise students to try out the plain square stance first, with the ball either opposite the left heel or just inside it. Modifications may start from this position, which is entirely orthodox, and seems suited to the greatest number of players. Of course individual peculiarities eventually will settle the individual style.

I sometimes think too much importance is given the exact stance by the average student. It is important, certainly, but not to an eighth of an inch. One thing you must be sure of—that the stance is comfortable and that you feel you can hit the ball from it.

Lesson III—Putting

I am not absolutely sure that golf for a great many years has not been taught wrong end first; that is, the full shot with a wood club being a pupil's introduction to the most complicated study in the world of sport. Naturally, the "big shot" appeals to the beginner; he wants most of all to see the ball get up and ride. But I doubt if that is the best thing for him to try to learn first. Perhaps it is too much like trying to teach a piano-pupil to play sonatas before he has learned to play scales. Anyway, the little shots should be practically miniature replicas of the big ones, and the tiny swing a segment of the great swing, and of course the putting swing is smallest of all, requiring less exertion of strength, and moving at less speed. Thus it should be easier to master at first, and we will take it up at the beginning.

As I said in the first chapter, putting is a game within a game, and the putting grip should not be exactly the same as the grip for other shots. So, too, the stance is likely to be different. Indeed, there is no really orthodox stance for putting, though there are methods that make putting more sure and safe.

The main thing about the putting stance and grip and swing is to arrange them so that the club is moving in an absolutely straight line toward the hole as the ball is struck. The "follow-through" you hear so much about does not mean the course of the clubhead after the ball is struck; that is the "finish." The follow-through

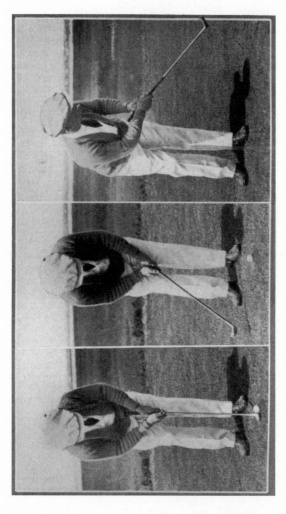

A Lesson in Golf-Putting. Famous teacher of Bobby Jones tells how to putt—errors of players explained. How to putt—first the address; second the back stroke, and third the follow-through or finish. Note the delicate grip and the wrist movement. In the putting stroke, the wrists are exactly opposed—the palms held facing one another—and the club sent on through the ball straight down the line of the putt. The back swing here is for a putt of twenty feet.

BOBBY JONES'S PUTTING STANCE
WAS MODELED ON KILTIE'S.

is the course of the clubhead while the club and the ball are in contact; and in putting, and in all other normal shots, the path should be a straight line during that contact.

In the putting grip, the hands should have the palms facing each other, so that the two wrists work as a hinge, backward and forward, along the line of the putt. The normal grip for a full shot will not accomplish this, for obvious reasons, the left hand being more on top of the shaft. The club must be held lightly and delicately; it is impossible to have a "putting touch" while squeezing the shaft, just as a billiardist would find it impossible to execute a proper stroke except with the cue held lightly in the fingers.

I advise that the feet be slightly apart and most of the weight on the left; it should not be equally distributed in any event as that gives a tendency to sway, and the body must be fixed and immovable in the putting stroke.

The putting stroke is essentially a "one-hand" stroke. You may make it with either hand; most players prefer the right; but it must be done with one or the other. By "stroke" here I mean the motion that sends the club on to the ball. Bob Jones takes the club back with his left hand and sends it on the ball with the right. He makes so much of a right-hand stroke of the putt that he reverses his grip for it, overlapping his right little finger with his left forefinger, instead of placing the right little finger over the left forefinger as in the other shots.

A slow backswing, just far enough to get the ball to the hole with a firm stroke, and perfect smoothness are essential. Never take the club back farther than is necessary, for all golf strokes must be firm and crisp. Send the club on toward the hole as the ball is struck, and watch the club strike it. Looking up too soon is just as ruinous in a short putt as in any other shot; maybe more so, for a missed drive may be retrieved but a short putt missed is a stroke gone.

Some general observations about putting may be in order, for it usually is the decisive factor in competitive play, since all great players, and all players of approximately the same class, will get to the green about alike. The critics emphasize the value of putting, and Walter Hagen, to go no farther, owes a major part of his great success to his fine and reliable putting.

It seems too obvious to mention that the ball should be sent as far as the cup, yet many otherwise good golfers never seem to get over a sort of timidity in their approach putts. Certainly if the ball does not reach the cup it will not drop, so it is well to make up your mind firmly to be past the hole on all putts, unless you are below it on a sloping green and need to get down in two, in which case it is unwise to run past to the uphill side. But in all putts you need to sink, putt for the back of the cup—putt to make the ball hit the back of it, especially on a rough or untrue green, since a ball firmly struck holds the line better than one merely trickled. On a keen, true green, you may remember that the cup has four "doors" and that a ball that just reaches the rim is likely to drop from either side, or even the back, as well as in the exact front. But this is a delicate point, and the general practice is to make the ball hit the back of the cup. If it won't drop then you at least have done your duty—you have given it a chance; and it is an odd fact that a golfer feels more uncertain in making a second putt from a foot short of the cup than in making it from two feet past; he seems to feel guilty over his timidity, and it is only too likely to affect his next stroke.

Lesson IV—The Chip Shot

The chip shot has been called the great economist of golf, and I do think it saves more strokes than any other, for the golfer who can command it. The chip shot takes up the slack, enabling you to get down in two from somewhere near the green after you have just failed to reach the green with the previous shot. Different experts play it in somewhat varied ways. Walter Hagen, who couples a fine putting method with an exceptionally good and reliable chip shot, uses four clubs for it, depending on the proportion of "chip," or flight in the air, and roll he desires. If he is well off the green, or with rough grass between him and the edge, and the hole is near that side, Hagen does not hesitate to use a mashie-niblick, getting the ball perhaps two-thirds of the way in the air with a correspondingly short roll. He uses the mashie for less flight and about an equal roll; and a No. 4 or a No. 3 iron for more roll and less flight. Bob Jones ordinarily plays the chip shot with a No. 3 iron, which is laid back a little more than a mid-iron. The plain mashie or the old-fashioned jigger is a good club for the shot.

As I play the chip shot, using a mashie almost exclusively, I have two different methods, depending on the proportion of chip and roll. One may be called the plain chip-and-run, or normal chip shot. The other is a sort of chip-and-drag, with more flight and trifle of backspin on the ball to check its roll.

I play the chip shot from almost a putting stance, feet fairly close together, weight mostly on the left foot. The

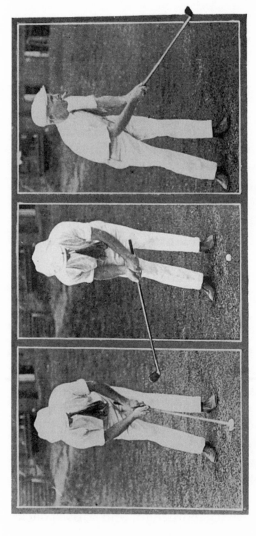

A Lesson in Golf—The Chip Shot. Great teacher tells how to make one of finest shots in all of golf—a real winner. Here we have three phases of the normal chip-shot, as played by Stewart Maiden. It is noted that the weight is on the left foot and the hands ahead of the clubhead in the address. This is for the true chip-and-run. For the "chip-and-drag," with more chip and less run, the weight is more back on the right foot, the hands are back of the clubhead in the address, and the stroke cuts slightly across the line of play, instead of hitting the ball right in the back. Mr. Maiden plays only those two types, which he says are enough for all purposes.

knees are not so rigid or the body as immovable as in the putt. Some teachers recommend this rigidity but I am not in agreement. There should be no exaggerated knee action, or hip movement, certainly; but enough flexibility and "play" to permit smoothness and ease in the stroke.

In the plain chip-and-run, used under all circum-stances where there is no rough grass or hazard to carry, I play the ball opposite the left heel with the hands in the address held pretty well ahead of the ball, the hands well down on the shaft, and a normal grip. The chip is played crisply, the ball being hit right "in the back," and the clubhead just snipping the grass under it and being sent through firmly toward the hole. Some people have the erroneous idea that "chip" implies chipping into the turf; this is an entirely different shot that need not be dis-cussed here, save to say that sometimes it has to be played from a bad lie; it really is a wee pitch with backspin.

The club is sent through the stroke mainly with the right hand and the blade turns normally away from the ball in the backswing and normally toward it and on over to the left as the club strikes the ball and contin-ues to the finish, which should find the club pointing almost directly at the hole.

In the chip-and-drag, the weight is more on the right foot and the hands at the address are rather back of the ball. This makes some important changes in the stroke. The loft of the club is made greater; there is a higher and longer flight for the ball; and a suspicion of back-spin is applied, permitting less roll.

In both types, the hands are well swung, with little or no "break" to the wrists. You will ruin the shot by trying to make a "wrist-shot" out of it, or if you take the club back farther than is necessary and try to "spare" the stroke as you come on the ball. Always hit firmly and crisply.

Lesson V—The Medium Pitch

Approaches to the green longer than those of the chip shot variety ordinarily are pitches of some sort, until we get into the department of iron play, which will be considered later. The first type of pitch shot I wish to present is the medium pitch, for a distance of 60 to 120 yards. There are a number of methods of playing this shot—the straight, firmly "knocked-down" shot with a powerful backspin, as it is played by Bob Jones and many other experts; the cut shot with sidespin as well as backspin; and the plain pitch with only the normal spin applied by the loft of the club. I shall give the method I regard as most reliable for the student, who of course will develop a more severe style as he progresses in the game, if he finds a need for it. I have not mentioned the pitch-and-run shot, valuable as it is, because the method I am going to explain includes this useful shot, which, by the way, is not so useful in America as it was 20 years ago, before the greens were so closely trapped as not often to permit much run of the ball after it lands.

The medium pitch, as I play it, is executed with a plain mashie, but many students will prefer the useful "spade" mashie or even a mashie-niblick. The same method will answer for either.

The stance should be moderately open and the ball well forward, in front of the left heel rather than back of it. I play it opposite the middle of the left foot. The weight is mostly on the right foot and the hands are

A Lesson in Golf—The Medium Pitch. Second step in approaching described—Maiden's personal style is distinctive. For the medium pitch, as played by Stewart Maiden, the ball is opposite the middle of the left foot, the weight of the player well back on the right foot, and the hands slightly back of the ball in the address. This gives the normal loft of the club, which in this case is a plain mashie. No. 1 shows the address. No. 2 is a rear view of the backswing, showing the straight left arm and clubface turned away from the ball. No. 3 is the finish, showing how the clubhead has been sent straight down the line of flight and now points toward the hole. (Note: The club, Mr. Maiden explains, does not stop in this position but continues normally upward to an easy and unrestricted finish.) The shot thus illustrated is of 100 yards, the ball stopping with a short roll after touching the green.

held the least bit back of the ball. This method gives the shot the benefit of the natural loft of the club and is very different from the "knock-down," turf-taking stroke that imparts strong backspin by reason of the club's face being still moving downward as the ball is struck. The stroke I am here describing is gauged so that the ball is taken almost exactly at the bottom of the swing; perhaps the least bit before, but not enough to figure on. Little or no turf is taken; the grass simply is snipped from just in front of where the ball lay. In a word, the ball is hit squarely in the back with a lofted club and naturally is pitched up into the air with a certain amount of backspin or reverse English—enough to check its roll within reasonable limits. It is the simplest pitch I know, and comes between the so-called pitch-and-run and the severe backspin pitch designed to stop the ball approximately where it lands.

The wrists are held firm throughout the stroke. The left arm must be straight all through the backswing and until after the ball has gone. The club should be sent straight down the line of the shot, the hands going through freely and unchecked, and not being turned over to the left, as they naturally finish in a full shot. The club's face is to be kept presented straight toward the ball as they come together; any suspicion of turning over the hands or rolling the wrists would put the shot off line to the left, probably with a pull. And again—do not take the club back any farther than is necessary to send the ball the required distance, so you can hit hard and hit crisply. A backswing that is too long means a flabby stroke, and that spells disaster in pitching, and in any other shot. Do not try to think of details during the stroke. Make up your mind completely before the swing is started, and after it starts think of only one thing— hit the ball!

Lesson VI—The Full Pitch

The full pitch, as I am about to explain it, differs from the medium pitch principally in the position of the ball and the distribution of the player's weight, as far as the method is concerned. It gives the ball a relatively lower flight, with greater range, and at the same time imparts more backspin, so that on landing it should stop more quickly. For the average masculine player, the full pitch with a mashie should mean a shot of from 120 to 150 yards; for a woman, from 100 to 130 yards.

For the full pitch, the ball should be played well inside the left heel, and the player's weight should be more on the left foot, instead of on the right. In addressing the ball, the hands are a little in front of it. These three mechanical differences from the medium pitch, with the same stroke, will give a quite different result. The combination of weight on the left foot, hands ahead of the ball, and ball back of the left heel takes some of the natural loft from the club and adjusts the bottom of the swing to a point some two inches ahead of the ball. This naturally brings the clubhead onto the ball while it still is moving downward as well as forward, and a considerable strip of turf or "divot" will be cut up just ahead of where the ball lay—a sort of proof that the stroke was properly made.

Since the club's normal loft is reduced by this method, the ball will fly lower and farther, the force of the stroke being more concentrated toward the objective. You might expect this also to supply a long run at the end of the flight, but this is where the increased backspin takes effect. Being rather knocked down by the descending club, the ball gets a severe wrench from the club's face, to which it sticks long enough to start spinning rapidly in a direction opposite to the line of flight. This spin does two things for the shot. It sustains the ball longer in the air, actually holding it up against the force of gravity until the flight is nearly over; and on touching the turf the backspin takes hold and grips, stopping the roll with surprising abruptness when the shot is properly made.

This is a simple matter of mechanics. There is nothing at all mysterious about the application of backspin, and the player does not have to do anything out of the ordinary with the club—simply hit the ball hard and firmly and crisply. The club does the rest. One great difficulty with many players is that they refuse to leave enough of the shot to the club.

The stroke for this shot rarely is a really full swing, where the club is taken back to the horizontal. Usually a three-quarters swing is sufficient. The left arm is kept straight all through; the club's face turns away from the ball as the backswing gets under way; at the top of the swing both hands are under the club, and both wrists well cocked or bent; the right elbow is kept fairly close to the ribs; and of course the weight goes forward onto the left foot as the ball is struck, finishing practically all on that foot. But these details must be worked out in practice swings with no ball to bother about. Once a real shot is started, all the players's concentration must be on one thing: hitting the ball.

For varying ranges, this shot may be played with any pitching club from a mashie-niblick to a No.4 iron.

Lesson VII—The Iron Shot

The "iron range," or the distance between the full mashie shot and the wood clubs, is a problem met in two ways, according to the preference of the experienced golfer. One school, rapidly diminishing but still numbering some very fine players in its ranks—Chick Evans is a good example—uses few irons and plays a variety of shots with each. At one recent championship Chick Evans was using only one iron, a mid iron (approximately a No. 2), and was playing shots of from 165 to 190 yards with it. The other school goes in for graduated irons, with a range for each club, the No. 4 iron having a range 15 or 20 yards greater than the mashie limit, and progressing on to the No. 1 iron that approximates the older-fashioned driving iron or cleek. No. 2 is the mid iron, the old reliable standby of the game. No. 3 has more loft, but less than the No. 4 or mashie-iron as it used to be called. For a good, strong masculine player, the ranges are about as follows: No. 4, 170 yards limit; No. 3, 180 yards; No. 2, 190 yards; and No. 1, 200 yards or a bit more in an emergency or downwind. Some very powerful iron players, like Bob Gardner, will take a No. 1 iron for a shot of 220 yards. It was with a No. 1 iron that Bob Jones played his most famous shot—the iron to seven feet from the pin from a distance of about 200 yards over a lagoon guarding the last green at Inwood, when he won the play-off for the Open championship with Bobby Cruickshank in 1923.

Personally, I like the use of four graduated irons and

A Lesson in Golf—The Iron Shot. Two styles of play with irons are described by famous teacher. This is the long-range iron shot played by Stewart Maiden, who in his own personal method does not favor "half" or "three-quarter" shots, but employs a series of irons, with each of which he plays two distinct types of shot, as described in the accompanying article.

usually teach it. In my opinion it is much simpler and easier to take a club that will just yield the range required and hit the ball hard than to take a club of less power and play a spared shot.

The accompanying illustrations are of a full shot to the green with a No. 4 iron and they serve for all my full iron shots; I am not conscious of any marked difference with the other irons.

As in the full pitch, I play the ball slightly back of the line of the left heel, with the hands a little in front of it at the address, and with the weight slightly more on the left foot, making it somewhat a downward blow onto the ball. This means that a small chip of turf or divot is taken in front of where the ball lies. This stroke gives the maximum of flight with a comparatively short roll, though it is by no means the special type known as the "push shot," which is a matter for advanced players.

Note that the hands are lifted high—as high as the head—that the club's face is opened well, turning away from the ball so that at the top of the swing the club's toe is pointing directly at the ground; the left heel is raised only as much as will admit of the club being taken back with a free pivot; the hips well turned—this is a part of the pivot—and the shoulders with them so that at the top of the swing the back is presented squarely down the line of the shot. The feet are kept planted as firmly as possible all through the backward and forward swing until the ball has gone; then, with the right arm keeping pace with the right leg, the right heel comes up as the weight goes forward, to finish well on the left foot.

Another type of full iron shot, higher and with less range, is played with the same swing exactly, only the ball is a little farther forward, nearly off the left heel, the weight is more on the right foot, and the hands are opposite the ball or a little back of it in the address. This stroke applies the club so that it takes the ball fairly in the back, giving it the benefit of all the natural loft of the club, and applying less backspin, more nearly resembling a pitched shot with all irons.

No iron club should be taken back beyond the horizontal and as a general rule the greater the loft of the club, the shorter the swing. The left arm is kept straight all through the stroke until the ball has gone; if any of the pictures show what seems to be a bend in that arm, the reason is having to stop and hold the position momentarily for the picture to be made. While some fine players may ease the elbow a trifle at the top of the swing, I think it the best practice to keep the arm straight, as it must be straightened out anyway before the club comes on the ball. Bob Jones keeps his left arm perfectly straight all through his full shots, until the ball has gone, and nearly all the great players of my acquaintance do likewise.

Iron play in a way is the backbone of a golfing style, and too much attention cannot be given it. But all the details here explained should be worked out and perfected in practice, and when a real shot is being played the mind should be free of every other consideration than of hitting the ball. This point cannot be emphasized too strongly.

Lesson VIII—Wood Club Play

Most beginners in golf get the idea that play with the iron clubs and play with the wood clubs is a radically different business, and every now and then a pupil will tell me: "As I understand it, you hit the ball with an iron and sweep it away with a wood club." This usually means he has been reading something highly theoretical about golf; there is plenty of theory to read, these days. As I understand it, and as I teach the game, and play the shots myself, there is no difference between the stroke with a wood club and the stroke with an iron, except the difference mechanically made necessary by the wood club being considerably longer in the shaft with a trifle more resiliency about it. Naturally, with a longer club, you stand farther from the ball. The old method of determining the approximate distance to stand from the ball with any club was to sole the club back of the ball and take a stance that just permitted the end of the shaft to touch the left knee, when it was bent a trifle forward. This in a general way is near enough right.

Wood clubs feel somewhat different from irons, since the latter are both shorter and heavier and their shafts are thicker and stiffer. The "lie" of course is flatter, too, since the player must stand farther from the ball.

As with the irons, I play two distinct kinds of full shot with the spoon, the brassie, and the driver. For the full range to be got from either of the three, I play the ball opposite my left heel with slightly more weight on

This is the address and top of the swing for a full spoon shot, which Maiden executes in the same manner as a brassie shot or a drive. The hands are held low at the address, and at the top of the swing the left heel is barely off the turf, the right elbow is close to the side, the left arm is straight, and the toe of the club pointing toward the ground.

BOBBY JONES'S ADDRESS.

the left foot at the address and the hands held a little in front of the ball as the stroke is started. This automatically tends to keep the ball low, applies a modicum of backspin, and thus gives it a long flight and a restricted roll. I do not play any full shot with iron or wood for intentional roll, though I know some fine players who impart a slight right-to-left spin on their tee shots—a tail-end pull or draw, it is called—to gain added distance with a long run. As a rule, that is a part of their method that is acquired more or less unconsciously and it is not wise for a beginner to strive for it.

The stance for a full wood shot is nearly square, as I play it, the left foot being just a shade back of the line of the right, but not enough to constitute the open stance. The hands are kept markedly low in the address; a point I would stress for all shots; Bob Jones, whose style is regarded as the best, holds his hands closer to his knees in the address than any other golfer I know. There should be a noticeable angle between the arms and the club-shaft in the address; nothing is weaker than having arms and shaft in one continuous line. My swing, and the one I believe to be most practical, is neither "flat" nor "upright"; the club is moving toward the back of the neck when the top of the swing is reached; and it is best not to allow it to droop below the horizontal, in which case it must be raised again before any speed is imparted to the stroke, or else the danger of hitting too soon—before the ball is reached—is exaggerated. Some very fine players take longer swings, but they have been doing it since childhood and it is a part of their style. You can hit just as hard from the horizontal and the shorter swing is more reliable.

One point I would stress in all full shots, with iron or wood. Many beginners, apparently having studied photographs of experts in action, get the notion that the left heel should be cocked up high as soon as the backswing is started—that the elevation of this heel is a primary part of the stroke. It is a part, but it is a result and not a cause. The left heel should not come off the turf until the backward turn of the body fairly pulls it from the ground, and it should not come up a fraction of an inch more than is necessary for pivoting. The left knee knuckles inward, and the left foot rather rocks in the same direction, instead of the heel being elevated as a separate motion. The left foot always should maintain a strong and substantial contact with the ground, even at the very top of the swing. This is absolutely essential.

It is rather the fashion nowadays to use only one club for tee shots and for the longest shots through the green, and many fine players carry only a brassie for these shots. It is simpler to employ one club for all wood shots except of the spoon or baffy type, and by using a low tee—I never have favored high ones—the similarity is kept more strictly, so that the shots may be played with as near the same feeling as possible. The spoon is an essential club, giving a steeper shot with less range, and the baffy, with its well-lofted face, is a favorite with many, though personally I do not care for it, using the spoon instead.

Lesson IX—Hip Action

I always have been against the idea of taking the swing to pieces and trying to tell a pupil how to do it by sec-tions, and certainly there can be no greater handicap in golf than for a player to analyze his stroke and play his shots while attempting to think about the various de-tails—how he starts the club back and when he turns his wrists, and how he starts the downswing; that sort of thing. Hitting a golf ball should be very much like throwing—not hitting—a baseball. And can you imag-ine a pitcher thinking about how he is going to wind up, and when he is going to bring his left foot down, and when he is going to let his wrist snap and cut the ball loose? He simply decides if he is going to pitch a fast ball or a curve, and whether high or low, and over which corner of the plate, and then he cuts loose. If he tried to think about pivoting or when to snap his wrist he would set a record for bases on balls and wild pitches, if the manager left him in there long enough.

Still, the golf swing is with an implement instead of with merely an arm, and it is more complicated than the pitching swing, and we have to consider some phases of it and get them right in order that the other phases may follow naturally and correctly. And the only one I am going to explain in these lessons to any extent is hip action.

No good golf shot at the full range ever was played without hip action; it means both range and control; and George Duncan, one of the greatest players as well as one of the smartest theorists of golf, has said that the secret of the good golf swing is the "sling" that starts with the left hip and draws the arms down and the body around, and brings the club onto the ball, in one smooth, rhythmic motion with the snap just at the right place. In the following chapter I shall consider timing, and it is just as well to explain here that in my system, timing starts with, and is largely controlled by, the hip action.

After the club is taken back for a full shot, or for any shot with power in it, the important point is to start the downward swing properly. This is done by starting the left hip and the left shoulder together, drawing down the arms with the hands practically in the same position as at the top of the swing until they are about the hip level. There is where the real "hit" begins, and at that stage the left hip has been sent forward along the line of the shot, establishing tension through all the left side of the body; the right knee is beginning to knuckle in toward the ball, and the right heel is rising from the ground. If you will take this position, as shown in the picture, you will feel the tension and the sense of power and a certain readiness for the hands to whip the club through with the wrists turning over automatically. Of course you cannot think of all these things during a stroke. But you must start working it out by leading with the left hip, for without its movement along the line of the shot, and the resultant "sling" and snap imparted to the stroke as the ball is taken, there can be no such thing as a powerful, long, or perfect golf shot. You will see that the club's face in the picture still is turned away from the ball as at the top of the swing. It is the returning of it to the ball that constitutes the "flick" or lash in the stroke, but it is the hip action that starts the swing properly and prepares the player for unwinding the wrists and for the successful completion of the stroke.

Lesson X—Timing

Speaking in the most general way, I should say that timing, the main factor in a golf stroke, is less mechanics than a state of mind, and this makes it difficult to explain. There is no photograph that will adequately picture a state of mind, and I shall have to hunt up some words. In a way, timing is what you require to crack a whip, or—to make it more homely and simple—to snap a towel against the most convenient portion of some friend's anatomy in the dressing room. Without any conscious mental process beyond treating him to a sharp sting, you draw back the towel and swing it forward, and just at the right juncture draw your hand back in such a manner as to snap the towel as it touches the victim of your crude brand of humor. You could not sting your friend by swinging the towel against him, no matter how much force you put into the swing, It is the snap that stings. And that is the secret of timing in the golfing stroke—not just swinging the clubhead against the ball, but snapping it against the ball and stinging it.

The most common violation of timing in a golf shot is hitting too soon; that is, delivering the snap, if any, before the club reaches the ball. I should say that hitting too soon spoils more golf shots than any other one fault; perhaps more than all the rest put together. By this error the ball may be smothered, topped, pushed out, sliced, hooked, swung to the left, or schlaffed—which is about all the things that can be done to a golf ball beside hitting it straight and far down the fairway.

Nor is this all. Many a player seems to be hitting the ball squarely in the back and sending it straight, but without power and with little range, and he is at a loss to account for his lack of yardage.

The explanation is easy. The "kick" in the stroke has been discharged before the club gets to the ball, and all the ball gets is a hangover.

When I said that timing was more a state of mind than mechanics, I did not mean that timing was without its mechanics. I suppose they are many and complex. But no player who ever lived could acquire timing by a study of its mechanics, even if he could learn to perform them properly and in sequence, without the state of mind that directs him simply to snap the clubhead against the ball. I would rather try to impart the state of mind and the mental impulse thus to lash the ball, and trust the mechanics to follow naturally and take care of themselves.

There is no set cue for timing that I am aware of. I fancy the projection of the left hip to its fullest reach along the line of the shot is the start of the hit, but that has to be an unconscious move that comes from the sense of timing.

I would warn the player against any effort to bat the ball away by means of force transmitted through the shaft of the club, as if pushing the clubhead against the ball; the shaft is only a connection between the clubhead and the hands, to enable the player to speed up the clubhead; and it is the speed at which the clubhead is moving as it takes the ball, and not the power used for the swing, that gives the distance. That is why some small and slight players can hit a ball much farther than big, powerful ones. It is the whiplash principle of the towel again; the snap, and not the swing, that stings and does the trick.

Bobby Jones called him "The First Doctor of Golf"

FAR to the front in the game's Hall of Fame belongs the name of Stewart Maiden. On the cobbles of the little sea-level village of Carnoustie, in Scotland, as a barefoot boy in wee kilties, he batted home-made cork balls with improvised sticks. And acquired the nickname "Kilty", which has adhered to him ever since. For companions he had half a dozen other boys who have since also become famous, some of them champions, in America. • • • • • • • • • •

He ventured West on a two-week voyage—found handfuls of golfers arriving in buggies at a handful of courses—became Pro at Wee Burn. Later he settled down at East Lake, Atlanta, and made the course world-famous.

The utterly phenomenal Bobby Jones and the 3-time Women's Champion, Alexia Ster-ling, he taught. In that interesting chronicle,

"Down the Fairway" . . . "I wasn't satisfied with the somewhat compromised style in which I was hitting the irons," says Bobby Jones. "I went out and had a little talk with Stewart Maiden, who to me will always be the first Doctor of Golf. I did a little con-fessing. 'Let's see you hit a few', said Stewart. I hit a few. Stewart seemed to be watching my right side. 'Move that right foot and shoulder back a bit', said Stewart. I did so, taking a square stance. 'Now what do I do?' I asked Stewart. 'Knock hell out of it!'—he is a man of few words. I did. The ball went on a line."

—And so they serve. • • •

"Kilty", and his lovable brother Jim, of the Nassau Country Club, are two more of the men to whom present-day America owes a lasting debt of gratitude for their great influence on a great game.

Wilson
GOLF EQUIPMENT
WILSON-WESTERN SPORTING GOODS CO. ◂ ◂ ◂ NEW YORK ◂ CHICAGO ◂ SAN FRANCISCO

THE THREE ESSENTIALS OF BETTER GOLF

Stewart Maiden

I have been teaching golf for more than 20 years. I have taught all kinds of golfers, from the veriest dub to the Champion of Champions, the only player who ever won the four major tournaments of golf the same year—British Open and Amateur and United States Open and Amateur—and I am convinced that golf is the simplest game in the world and, at the same time, the hardest game in the world. It is simple, provided three essentials are observed; it is hard, if those fundamentals are ignored.

The greater part of my teaching has been of golfers who have already started the game, have been fascinated by it, and want to improve. They come to me for instruction and my work has been made doubly difficult through the fact that I must begin by tearing down. I must seek to eradicate mistakes that have crept in, try to make the golfer unlearn a lot of nonessential things, and get him started right, namely, thinking of the golf stroke as it should be made.

What are the three essentials to Better Golf? They are:

1. Right Balance.

2. Right Grip.

3. Right Clubs.

The Right Balance

By right balance, I mean a "flowing balance," as opposed to a static balance. It is the balance one has in walking, nothing more or less. In walking one is on the balls of his feet, his weight well forward. In standing still one is on the heels, the weight well back. With the weight on the heels it is hard to make the golf stroke correctly.

In addressing the ball you should have the weight evenly divided between the left foot and the right foot, but the tendency should be toward "leaning forward" rather than the reverse. If your weight is on the heels, your tendency is to turn the shoulders without any pivot at the hips, and the whole shot is spoiled. Then again, when the weight is on the heels, there is a tendency to tighten the leg muscles, and nothing is more fatal to the correct golf swing than stiff legs. So the first thought I would try to impress on any golfer is the idea of right balance, a flowing balance, such as one preserves in walking, muscles flexed and not taut.

The Right Grip

When I speak of the right grip I am not unmindful of the fact that there are almost as many grips as there are golfers and that golfers have achieved great successes using an unorthodox grip. Yet my observation leads me to believe that the grip is the most important thing in golf, next to correct balance, and that unless the grip is right, difficulties that are enormous face the player.

The grip I prefer is the overlapping grip, the one now used in some form or another by perhaps 90 percent of all golfers. With this grip the left hand grasps the club partly in the palm, so that the left thumb is down the right side of the shaft, rather than on top. The grip is largely with the last three fingers of the left hand, and the right hand is applied so that the little finger of the right hand overlaps, rides on the forefinger of the left hand, and the grip with the right hand is with the first three fingers. Mark this difference. The grip with the left hand is with the last three fingers; with the right hand the first three fingers.

Having the right grip enables a golfer to get the proper hand and wrist action at the top of the swing. If he uses some other grip, notably the palm grip throughout, he must make adjustments in his swing to compensate. So I would urge beginning golfers to start right, to get the right idea of balance and to get the right grip—then all the rest will come easy.

The Right Clubs

When I was asked to design a set of clubs that would be correct for 90 percent of golfers, I hesitated because I had had experience in selecting golf clubs for my pupils and knew how difficult it was to get a set of clubs, matched in all particulars. I knew the years that some of my pupils had spent in picking up here and there clubs that were of first one make and then another, that were not matched as far as appearance is concerned, but were matched in the essential factors that go to make up a perfect matched set. I doubted the ability of any organization to turn out clubs according to my ideals.

But then I didn't know about the Hillerich & Bradsby organization. When I went to the factory in Louisville, I found an organization that played golf, knew golf, and understood what golf clubs should be. The factory gave

STEWART MAIDEN SHARING HIS CLUBMAKING KNOW-
LEDGE.

me every assistance and I have designed a set of clubs
that I believe are as near perfect as it is possible for
clubs to be.

I think those who know me know that I would not
lend my name to any enterprise that I did not believe
in thoroughly. I actually designed the clubs that bear
my name, designed them out of my rich experience of
years in teaching golf and fitting players with golf clubs.
You can buy lots of clubs more dolled up than these are,
and for less money, but I don't believe you will find anywhere sets of clubs that are more correct from the playability angle, or whose lines promote so effectually the
confidence that is so essential to good golf.

There are certain features about these clubs that are noteworthy. In the first place, the lines inspire confidence. You feel when you address the ball that you are going to hit it far and hit it straight. Lots of clubs are built with a slant to the right or a slant to the left, so that a golfer must make adjustments, he must let the club play him, rather than play the club. I don't think a golfer will meet with this difficulty in playing the clubs that bear my name.

Why Clubs with Flat Lies

The golfer will notice that the clubs carrying my name are slightly on the "flat" side, as regards lie. They are made that way deliberately. My long experience in teaching convinces me that it is much easier to play with a flat lie than with an upright lie. Players can adjust themselves more easily to a club with a flat lie. Furthermore, with clubs of a flat lie a golfer can address the ball in the natural position of the hands, and with a straight left arm, not with the wrists arched up in front to suit the lie of the club.

Another thing about the clubs that is distinctive is that the blades are on the compact side and rather deep in the face. They have been made so designedly. The natural tendency of a golfer is to slice the ball. The deep face tends to counteract this. Conversely, if a golfer shows a tendency to hook the ball, I would recommend that he use shallow face clubs. But the fact that 75 percent of the golfers slice is reason enough why golf clubs built for the average golfer should have plenty of depth to them.

Now presuming you have the right set of clubs, clubs fitted to you according to the suggestions of the Stewart Maiden Golf Club Fitting Chart, that you have the Right

Use this Chart to Insure Getting Clubs That Fit

Sponsored by

Stewart Maiden

First Golf Instructor of Bobby Jones

THIS chart insures your getting Clubs fitted correctly to your physical type. Nine out of ten Golfers (all except those of exceptional physical types) can follow with confidence the instructions below. Your age, weight, height, and other physical characteristics are factors in determining what weight and length Golf Clubs will suit you best. All of these factors have been taken into consideration in the recommendations below but the two important factors are: PHYSICAL TYPE (normal, rugged, rotund). REACH (length of arms, obtained by measuring from knuckles to ground).

Then classify yourself as to physical type (normal, rugged, rotund). The cross index given by these two factors, Reach and Physical Type, (the square under your Physical Type and opposite your Reach measurement) tells you the specifications of Clubs that will fit you correctly.

EXAMPLE 1—Your Reach is 30 inches and you are of the Normal type. The square under Normal and opposite 30 inches shows that you should use wood Clubs 42½ inches long and weighing 12¾ to 13 ounces.

In Grand Slam indexed Irons, either the SM-2, TM-2, EM-2, AM-1, BM-1 or DM-1, as selected from catalog: the index being "M." In related Irons use ** (2 stars).

EXAMPLE 2—Your Reach is 32 inches and you are of the Rugged Type. The square under Rugged and opposite 32 inches shows that you should use wood Clubs 43 inches long and weighing 13 to 13¾ ounces.

In Grand Slam indexed Irons, either the SO-2, TO-2, EO-2, AO-1, BO-1 or DO-1, as selected from catalog: the index being "O.". In related Irons use *** (3 stars).

Make this measurement (Knuckles to Ground). This gives a guide to the length Clubs that will suit you best.

	NORMAL TYPE	RUGGED TYPE	ROTUND TYPE

NORMAL TYPE

Of average weight for height, medium size hands and wrists. In this group should be included the wiry type—Golfers somewhat below normal in weight as compared to height, but with good muscular development, younger men who have been active in athletics, and older men of this type who have played enough Golf to play with a fair degree of control. Above middle age, see Rotund Type.

RUGGED TYPE

Normal or slightly above the weight as compared to height, well developed muscularly—the football type—large hands and strong wrists. In this group should be included experienced Golfers of normal muscular development and weight who have developed something of a grooved swing.

ROTUND TYPE

Over-weight as compared to height, where excess weight checks physical activity. In this group should be included Golfers of Normal Type above middle age who would naturally lack normal control of muscles.

If the Golfer Measures

28
Inches from Knuckles to Ground

NORMAL: WOOD CLUBS. 41 inches; 12¾–13 oz. IRON CLUBS. Light-short Group. In Grand Slam indexed Irons with letter P as part of index—SP-2, TP-2, EP-2, AP-1, BP-1, DP-1. In related Irons those marked **** (4 stars).

RUGGED: WOOD CLUBS. 41 inches; 13–13¼ oz. IRON CLUBS. Standard Group. In Grand Slam indexed Irons with letter M as part of index—SM-2, TM-2, EM-2, AM-1, BM-1, DM-1. In related Irons those marked * (1 star).

ROTUND: WOOD CLUBS. 42 inches; 13¾–13¾ oz. IRON CLUBS. Light-short Group. In Grand Slam indexed Irons with letter P as part of index—SP-2, TP-2, EP-2, AP-1, BP-1, DP-1. In related Irons those marked * (1 star).

29
Inches

NORMAL: WOOD CLUBS. 42 inches; 12¾–13 oz. IRON CLUBS. Light-short Group. In Grand Slam indexed Irons with letter P as part of index—SP-2, TP-2, EP-2, AP-1, BP-1, DP-1. In related Irons those marked * (1 star).

RUGGED: WOOD CLUBS. 42 inches; 13¼–13¾ oz. IRON CLUBS. Standard Group. In Grand Slam indexed Irons with letter M as part of index—SM-2, TM-2, EM-2, AM-1, BM-1, DM-1. In related Irons those marked * (1 star).

ROTUND: WOOD CLUBS. 42 inches; 13¼–13¾ oz. IRON CLUBS. Standard Group. In Grand Slam indexed Irons with letter M as part of index—SM-2, TM-2, EM-2, AM-1, BM-1, DM-1. In related Irons those marked ** (1 star).

30
Inches

NORMAL: WOOD CLUBS. 42½ inches; 13–13¾ oz. IRON CLUBS. Standard Group. In Grand Slam indexed Irons with letter M as part of index—SM-2, TM-2, EM-2, AM-1, BM-1, DM-1. In related Irons those marked ** (2 stars).

RUGGED: WOOD CLUBS. 42½ inches; 13¼–13¾ oz. IRON CLUBS. Heavy Group. In Grand Slam indexed Irons with letter O as part of index—SO-2, TO-2, EO-2, AO-1, BO-1, DO-1. In related Irons those marked ** (2 stars).

ROTUND: WOOD CLUBS. 42½ inches; 13¼–13¾ oz. IRON CLUBS. Standard Group. In Grand Slam indexed Irons with letter M as part of index—SM-2, TM-2, EM-2, AM-1, BM-1, DM-1. In related Irons those marked ** (2 stars).

31
Inches

NORMAL: WOOD CLUBS. 42½ inches; 13–13¾ oz. IRON CLUBS. Standard Group. In Grand Slam indexed Irons with letter M as part of index—SM-2, TM-2, EM-2, AM-1, BM-1, DM-1. In related Irons those marked ** (2 stars).

RUGGED: WOOD CLUBS. 42½ inches; 13–13¾ oz. IRON CLUBS. Heavy Group. In Grand Slam indexed Irons with letter O as part of index—SO-2, TO-2, EO-2, AO-1, BO-1, DO-1. In related Irons those marked ** (2 stars).

ROTUND: WOOD CLUBS. 43 inches; 13½–13¾ oz. IRON CLUBS. Heavy Group. In Grand Slam indexed Irons with letter O as part of index—SO-2, TO-2, EO-2, AO-1, BO-1, DO-1. In related Irons those marked ** (2 stars).

32
Inches

NORMAL: WOOD CLUBS. 43 inches; 13–13¾ oz. IRON CLUBS. Long Group. In Grand Slam indexed Irons with letter N as part of index—SN-2, TN-2, EN-2, AN-1, BN-1, DN-1. In related Irons those marked *** (3 stars).

RUGGED: WOOD CLUBS. 43 inches; 13–13¾ oz. IRON CLUBS. Long Group. In Grand Slam indexed Irons with letter N as part of index—SN-2, TN-2, EN-2, AN-1, BO-1, DO-1. In related Irons those marked *** (3 stars).

ROTUND: WOOD CLUBS. 43 inches; 13½–13¾ oz. IRON CLUBS. Long Group. In Grand Slam indexed Irons with letter N as part of index—SN-2, TN-2, EN-2, AN-1, BN-1, DN-1. In related Irons those marked *** (3 stars).

33
Inches

NORMAL: WOOD CLUBS. 43 inches; 13–13¾ oz. IRON CLUBS. Long Group. In Grand Slam indexed Irons with letter N as part of index—SN-2, TN-2, EN-2, AN-1, BN-1, DN-1. In related Irons those marked **** (3 stars).

RUGGED: WOOD CLUBS. 43 inches; 13–13¾ oz. IRON CLUBS. Long Group. In Grand Slam indexed Irons with letter N as part of index—SN-2, TN-2, EN-2, AN-1, BN-1, DN-1. In related Irons those marked **** (3 stars).

ROTUND: WOOD CLUBS. 43 inches; 13¾–13¾ oz. IRON CLUBS. Long Group. In Grand Slam indexed Irons with letter N as part of index—SN-2, TN-2, EN-2, AN-1, BN-1, DN-1. In related Irons those marked **** (3 stars).

Grip and have firmly implanted in your mind the idea of the Right Balance, a flowing balance, not a static balance, we are ready to start our round and get a few pointers on how the various shots in golf should be played.

Essentially the method of playing the long shots in golf, that is, the drive, the brassie shot, the spoon shot, and the long iron shot, is the same. The shots differ in minor details of stance only, the swing is the same.

Tips on the Tee Shot

Conditions of the tee shot are less exacting than for any other shot in golf. The ball sits up; you can pick your own stance, within certain limits; there is less demand for exactness of direction. Therein lies its peril. The temptation to slug the ball is almost irresistible and restraint, which you will find is an important factor in golf, usually is lacking on the tee shot. Swing well within yourself; don't try to kill the ball. Remember that speed and accuracy of swing mean everything and that power is worthwhile only when it is translated into speed.

The following instructions apply to the drive, the brassie shot, the spoon shot, and the long irons.

Take your stance with the weight evenly distributed between the two feet and the weight inclined forward, toward the balls of the feet.

Hold the hands low, not stretched out in front of you. There must be a perceptible break at the wrists. The line formed by the shaft of the club and your left arm is not a straight line, but broken at the wrists.

Head over the ball and kept absolutely still until the ball is hit.

To start the swing, straighten out the right leg. Move the right hip and shoulder directly away from the ball.

Keep the left arm and hands close to the right knee. This will prevent the arms from swinging outside the proper line, and will encourage you to hit from the inside directly at the object you are aiming at—the ball.

Don't use the wrists to start the clubhead back. Start back with the arms without breaking the wrists. They do not break until the upward turn.

Always keep your body turned a little ahead of the club. If you don't, you will set up resistance to the swing of the arms when they start the upward turn and that means either a broken grip or a bent left arm and no wrist cock at the top of the swing, and the tension of the left arm and the left side, that is so necessary to start the forward motion of the hips on the downward swing, is sadly lacking.

Left Side Tension

This is an important point that deserves emphasis— the tension in the left arm and left side. It must be kept up to keep your body ahead of the stroke and clear the way for the arms to bring the club back to the ball without any resistance from the body. If there is any resistance set up to the force of your own blow, then balance, control, power, rhythm, everything that goes to make a perfect shot, is simply destroyed.

The hands and wrists perform their function at the bottom of the swing. Use them freely there with a throwing sort of feeling. There is no exact time or place in the downswing that one can say is the right time to use the wrists and hands, because we all feel differently. It must be done by "feel" alone. But you can be sure of one thing and that is, don't start it too soon.

For most tee shots, where there is no restriction on

the length to be obtained, the Driver is the correct club. For tee shots, where control of distance as well as direction is demanded, the length of shot governs the choice of club, which may be Driver, Brassie, Spoon, No. 1 Iron, or one of the other iron clubs.

One mistake the beginner is likely to make is to select a Driver that is on the long side, on the theory that length will increase the power of the blow. That is true within certain limits, but control of long clubs is more difficult and we must sacrifice something in distance for direction even on tee shots. I unhesitatingly recommend that the golfer follow the directions of the Stewart Maiden Golf Club Fitting Chart and he won't go far wrong as to the proper weight and the proper length of clubs.

The fairway shot with wood clubs is not essentially different from the tee wood shot. A mistake many players make is to think that some extra muscular twist is necessary to get the ball off the ground. If the ball is lying so close as that, you had better select a club with greater loft and be content with less distance. Swing Brassie and Spoon as you would your Driver and avoid trying to lift the ball. Let the greater loft of the clubs attend to that.

Remember what we have said about maintaining balance—a flowing rather than a static balance. Remember that the center or base of your swing is the head. If that moves, the foundation for the swing is broken up and you cannot get back where you started from. Your subconscious mind tells you when this point moves and instinctively you try to get it back in position by some shift in your swing—usually with disaster. That is why the old axiom, "Keep Your Head Still," is not only one of the oldest, but one of the most important, in golf. It could better be expressed, "Keep Your Balance."

Making Approach Shots

With approach shots, the goal is not merely to get a certain distance, but to reach and hold the green as near
as possible to the flag. Many players consider this the
most important shot in golf and rightly so. Long pitches
are played very much along the same line as the tee
shot except that the ball is played more toward the right
foot and is taken on a much straighter down angle. Hitting down on the ball produces backspin. Backspin
causes the ball to stop with little or no run. That is the
ideal on approach shots. Keep the ball in the air. As John
Henry Taylor said, "There are no bunkers in the air."
Really there is no mystery about applying backspin; it
is accomplished simply by hitting down on the ball and
any shot that you can hit hard enough to impart backspin to the ball is by far the easiest shot to play. I recommend that a golfer practice this shot consistently.

The swing with the iron clubs is more compact than
with the woods, for you must stand closer to the ball
and you do not carry the clubhead back quite so far.
There is less freedom, for, whereas with wood clubs you
are more concerned with distance than accuracy, with
iron clubs accuracy is the first consideration. Select the
proper club for the distance; you should learn your own
capabilities and, if there is any doubt in your mind as
to the proper club, select the more powerful one. Swing
well within yourself and concentrate on direction. However, don't make the mistake of trying to steer the ball.

Iron shots differ from wood shots in one other important particular. Whereas with the woods your effort
should be to sweep the ball from tee or fairway, just
grazing the turf, the stroke with the irons is a distinct
hit and the best players let the clubhead follow into the
turf just after it reaches the ball.

More about Backspin

But to revert to backspin and shots played with it. The approach shot that carries the green and pulls up with little or no run, and near enough to the flag to make getting down in one putt probable, is one of the most satisfying shots in golf. For these shots, usually ranging from 90 to 140 yards, modern golfers play to have the ball reach the green and stop; for longer shots the ball is played to hit short of the green and run on. It is with the Mashie (No. 5 Iron), the Spade Mashie (No. 6 Iron), and the Mashie-Niblick (No. 7 Iron) that the expert golfer can work his magic. There is not much choice in the driver of first rank golfers, but what a difference in the way their approach shots are played! You can always tell when an approach shot has been hit well. It leaves its trademark on the green. Examine one of these marks and you will note that a bit of turf has been rolled up by contact with the ball. It is the backspin on the ball that gives it this bite.

There are essentially four spins that a ball can take; a spin from left to right that usually gives a slice or curve to the right; a spin from right to left that brings about a hook or pull to the left of the proper line; a forward spin or overspin; and backspin. The first two are to be shunned, except when a player has progressed sufficiently to be able to pull or slice intentionally and can use these shots to avoid certain difficulties. The ball hit with a forward spin has less carry but a maximum of run. Control of distance is lacking.

But the ball hit properly with backspin carries farther and has little run. In fact with lofted clubs, it stops almost dead. Then, again, this backspin, which is imparted by "hitting down on the ball" (note that the ball is nearer the right foot than on tee shots), serves to impart a twist to the ball and holds it straight, just as the rifles of a gun help to hold the bullet straight. The golfer who is able to play his approach shots correctly— with backspin—should be able to hold his own in almost any company. "Control" of approach shots is the hallmark of a good golfer.

The Short Game

Up to the present we have been discussing full shots; that is, shots where the full power of the club is employed. There are other shots in golf that are vitally important. For instance, short shots of 30 to 50 yards. How are we going to play them?

Well, there are two ways, dictated by the circumstances. If there are difficulties in your path—bunkers—you have only one choice—a pitch. Short pitches of from 30 to 50 yards should be played well up off the left foot. Note the difference. With longer approach shots, where you can hit hard, play the ball back off the right foot and hit down on it. But when we come to the shorter shots we can't hit hard enough to impart the necessary backspin and we must get our stop another way. Now, please, follow the instructions carefully.

Take your stance so that the ball is opposite the left foot. Avoid turning the hips or perhaps it would be better to say, turn them only slightly, so that the club does not come too far inside the line of play. Turn the toe of the club slightly to the right, so as to open up the blade of the club, and hit across to the left of the line of play.

To play the pitch and run, just the reverse procedure is recommended. Play the ball back toward the right foot and have the clubface more or less closed. There is a slight turn of the hips and knees and the hands are well on the inside of the intended line of flight of the ball.

Chip shots around the green are played in exactly the same manner. If you want drag; that is, to have the ball stop quickly, play it up in front and open the face of the club at the address. Swing straight back or slightly on the outside and hit to the left. If you want overspin, want a ball that will roll, keep the ball back toward the right foot, with the clubface closed at the address and with the hands swinging on the inside of the line of play.

Here is a bit of advice that should be emphasized. In playing short shots, do not stand stiff or still; keep the knees in action, "as there is nothing more fatal than stiff legs." Avoid trying to make even the shortest shot with the wrists alone. Remember the hands and arms must swing back far enough to give you the power to hit with an easy flowing rhythm, rather than to hit with a short, quick jab. It is always easier to change the pace of your blow, provided your backswing is long enough to permit it.

The No. 9 Iron

For these short chip shots the more expert golfer uses a No. 4 iron, or the Mashie or the No. 6 Iron. For the golfer who knows his Bermudas, such a club is satisfactory, but extreme delicacy or touch and accuracy are required; if the swing is a little bit off, if the sharp blade digs into the turf too much, the shot is flubbed. The best club for the average golfer on shots of this character, that is, pitch-and-run approaches, is a slightly lofted club that can be played almost the same as a putter. The No. 9 Iron, or Approach Putter, is designed especially for shots of this kind. More lofted than a putter, it has approximately the same lie, permitting the player to stand close to the ball, and the shot is played almost the same way a long putt would be played. The ball pitches approximately one-third the distance to the hole and runs the rest of the way. And you will be surprised how often it is "dead."

The main advantage of the No. 9 Iron over a more lofted club is that the danger of the sharp blade digging into the turf too much is practically eliminated. The No. 9 Iron in my set of clubs has a heavy flange sole that gives solidity to the blow and promotes confidence.

Playing Bunker Shots

Bunker shots are played along the same lines as the chip shot. If the bunker is shallow and the lie good, play the ball from between the middle of the feet. Keep the hands and arms on the inside of the swing. Keep the clubhead coming up. Hit the ball on the downward swing. Hit the ball first and the sand afterward.

Where the bunker is deep with steep sides play the ball well off of the left foot, turn the toe of the club out, opening the blade. The steeper the bank, or the shorter the distance, the more you open the face of your club. Be sure to turn the body well to the left of the line of play. There is very little turn to the hips. Keep the arms well outside the line of play. The reason for this is so that you can hit straight across the ball. Swing freely and take plenty of sand behind the ball.

The essence of the explosion bunker shot is to take sand. The clubhead never touches the ball. The sand forms a cushion between ball and clubhead; as a result the ball has little or no run left when it hits the green. Govern the distance by the degree you open the blade and by the amount of sand you take.

Concerning Putting

I hesitate to write anything about putting, for there is no such thing as an orthodox method of putting. There is more opportunity for individuality in putting than in any other stroke in golf. Yet some suggestions may be helpful. First, get a comfortable stance. Use either the overlapping grip or the reverse overlap, in which the right hand grasps the club with all four fingers and the left forefinger overlaps, or rides, the little finger of the right hand. Do not stand so close to the ball that your eyes will have to focus at an angle; that is, looking back at your feet, but be sure they are looking away from your body and out toward the ball. Swing the hands on the inside of the angle. Keep the clubface closed. Do not try to keep the body still. There must be just a little give to the shoulders to provide a nice easy-flowing motion. Swing the club far enough back to give you time to swing, so that you do not have to hurry or force the club into a quick jerk or stab to get up enough speed into the swing.

Manifestly it is impossible in a booklet of this sort to go into great detail and explain how each shot should be played. Golf is so much a matter of muscular sensation, of "feel," that it is hard to describe the correct methods. Yet I hope that this little dissertation will accomplish its purpose and improve your game. I know it will, if you get to thinking of the golf swing in the right way. Remember the three essentials:

1. Right Balance.

2. Right Grip.

3. Right Clubs.

And finally, learn to play the shot with backspin correctly. Master that and you can qualify for an A.B., an A.M., or even a Ph.D. degree in golf.

A Word about Matched Sets

It is comparatively easy to build golf clubs that have the appearance of being matched; no special skill in designing or manufacturing is required; frills of ornamentation are available to anyone. Putting five, six, eight, or nine clubs in a box and labeling them "matched" does not necessarily produce matched clubs. To make the kind of clubs that really promote Better Golf requires not merely expert designing, selecting the best materials, painstaking workmanship, and exacting inspection; creating really matched and harmonized clubs means refining each club with the nicety of piano tuning so that each club in a set will be in tune with every other club and the whole set will be keyed to the physical type for which they are designed. To make such clubs is a task that can be trusted only to skilled artisans who play golf, who know what golf clubs should be, and how to build into them the unseen factors that provide 100 percent playability.

A visit to the factory where Stewart Maiden Grand Slam Indexed and Registered Clubs are produced would reveal an organization of golfers trained to produce 100 percent correct golf equipment:

- How the iron heads themselves, in addition to having correct lines, correct loft, correct lies, must have a definite balance.
- How checking with calipers assures exact adherence to the models designed by a clubsmith who learned his art in Scotland.

STEWART MAIDEN CLUBS MADE BY AND FOR HIM.

- How the heads are ground to definite weights to ensure proper relation in balance with the shaft.
- How the wood heads are carefully checked with the original patterns, revised by the leading clubmaker in America.
- How the shafts are bought; not so many shafts for wood clubs, and so many shafts for iron clubs, but of definite weights and degrees of stiffness, one weight and degree of stiffness for a Driver, another for a Spoon; one weight and degree of stiffness for a No. 2 Iron, another for a No. 6 Spade.
- How the shafts are tested, not merely for pos-

sible defects, but for resiliency, for comeback qualities, and weighed so that there will be the proper relation with the head to which a shaft is attached, the first step toward correct balance.

- How a special grade of leather is purchased for grips and how it receives special treatment to ensure the tacky feel that inspires confidence.
- How appearance factors are tested first for their effect on a club's playability and are added only as they will reflect more completely that playability.
- How special machines have been designed and built to do just one small operation that increases the assurance of perfect balance or correct shafting.
- How handwork at the bench follows machine turning to get shafts of exactly the correct weight and resiliency; with a master set before him the Grand Slam clubsmith builds each set to match in every feature the master specifications.

You would learn from this visit that in order to provide correct equipment for all types of golfers these matched sets are manufactured in four groups, roughly classified as Standard, Heavy, Long, and Light-Short, and that each group has its individual specifications as to weights of blades, lengths and weights of shafts, resiliency of shafts, balance points, and other details.

You would learn also that the unique Grand Slam method of building Indexed clubs not only provides clubs that are balanced, graduated for power, and harmonized for resiliency of shafts, but also offers the opportunity for a golfer to build up a matched set as he would a sectional filing system. They are offered regularly in sets of six, eight and ten clubs, but a golfer may start with four, if he desires, and later complete his set by adding the missing numbers carrying the same set index. This simple method of indexing also permits easy duplication of any club that may be lost.

Grand Slam Matched and Indexed Irons, designed by Stewart Maiden, are the finest products of the expert clubmaker's art. A golfer who chooses them can feel fully confident of their dependability—that they are built for him.

THE SILENT SCOT

FROM THE WRITINGS OF O.B. KEELER BY GRANTLAND RICE
"THE BOBBY JONES STORY"

Carnoustie is a dear little Scottish town, whose name is not unfamiliar in my home town, Atlanta, which has had upward of a dozen golf professionals from this small, Caledonian village. One was Willie Mann, dear old "Wullie," who was the first professional that the Druid Hills Golf Club had. There was Alex Smith, Jimmie Maiden and his brother Stewart, Kiltie the Kingmaker, and Willie Ogg and Charley Gray; all from Carnoustie, a town of 6,000 inhabitants and five golf courses; where an inexorable law says you may not play golf on the Sabbath day, and where the inhabitants carry curious little walking sticks on Sunday, the top fashioned in the shape of a golf clubhead, which they swing, meditatively, as they take their Sabbath evening walks.

Sunday was the Sabbath in most of Scotland. At St. Andrews, there was nae gowf on Sunday. It was suggested that there might be conceivably a bootleg sort o'gowf; a putting course, mind you, hid out in the low hills among the heather to which steal unobtrusively certain desperate addicts of the game, of a Sabbath afternoon; and jouk in amang the heather for a roond or twa on the wee links. But naething legal! They played gowf on Sunday at Gleneagles, which was an American and ungodly type of perfectly beautiful golfing resort. I was there twice and approved it thoroughly, especially the day Mr. Jones shot a 67.

Our visit to Carnoustie was a sort of pilgrimage, especially for Bobby, the home of his friend and mentor and the man who was responsible for his golf — Stewart Maiden. Bobby had just been crowned British Open Champion at St. Andrews for the second successive time, his name was ringing through the land, and he was going over to play an exhibition round on his teacher's old home course at Carnoustie.

Stewart was along of course, and George Low, who arranged the event. In all my experience in golf which has been certainly not brief and perhaps not inconsiderable, there is nothing that quite compares with that pilgrimage to Carnoustie across the Tay river from St. Andrews. Even Stewart, the taciturn Caledonian loosened up. We crossed the Tay on a ferry boat, and Stewart, spying a Scottish piper in full regalia, sidled off from the rest of the party, and the next thing we knew, the piper was strutting up and down the deck, and no true piper can pipe unless he is strutting, blowing "Cock of the North," quite lustily. He made them skirl with a will. My ambition heretofore had been to play a trombone or sliphorn, but right there, I was a convert to the bagpipe. But it needs a lot of room. It is strictly outdoor music.

At Dundee, the far side of the Tay, a thousand citizens, mysteriously apprised, were waiting to salute Bobby Jones, the unofficial King of Scotland. The way those people loved golf and Bobby is beyond words. It was ten minutes before his car could get started for Carnoustie. And there the mayor, or provost, awaited him with the key to the city and after luncheon, Bobby went out to play golf. About 6,000 of the population, which is estimated at 6,000, went along with him. I took a few pictures, then I found Stewart, and we turned back toward his old home.

I wished the boys from East Lake might have been along on this pilgrimage to visit the town and the golf course and Stewart's old home. We went along a substantial sort of street, all the houses of Scottish stone on both sides; low, solid, built for centuries. And we came to the home of Stewart Maiden. . . .

Stewart's mother was out in the little garden in the rear of the house and we spent an hour there. The dearest lady I have seen was Stewart's mother and I took a picture of her and Stewart on a bench in the garden. They thought a deal of Stewart, his mother and sister. And Stewart loved them no less.

It was a wonderful thing to see the way Stewart's fellow townsmen greeted him as we were walking about the golf course, or walking through the town.

Up came a big Caledonian who had not seen Stewart in 20 years.

"Aye, Stewart," said he, as if it had been 20 minutes.

"Aye, Wullie," said Stewart in the same unexcited tone.

And they talked, Wullie doing most of the talking until another Scot strolled up.

"Aye, Stewart," said the newcomer.

"Aye, Sandy," said Stewart and Sandy joined in the conversation.

Another with flaming red hair walked up.

"Aye, Stewart," said he.

"Aye, Red," said Stewart, and they all were talking, although I would say Wullie kept up his end rather thoroughly.

In five minutes six of Stewart's old cronies strolled up, unconcernedly. I gathered they had heard most completely the story of Stewart's success in America; and certainly they knew accurately the triumphs of his famous pupil. But there was a curious lack of demonstration.

"Aye, Stewart," they saluted him in his hometown. And "Aye, Sand," was the Silent Scot's rejoinder.

THE MOST COMMON FAULTS

Stewart Maiden As Told to O.B. Keeler

Interviewing Stewart Maiden is something of an undertaking. Few Scots are loquacious. This particularly applies to golfing Scots. Jock Hutchison, now, will talk on occasion. There is a certain Caledonian poem concerning one Jock McLean, a Hieland mon which The Hutch will recite with rare unction, properly approached. George Duncan also will talk fluently on practically every subject from a socketed mashie shot to the Theory of Evolution—and George has sound and substantial ideas on both. But in the main, Scots are reticent, and Stewart Maiden of East Lake, mentor unto Bobby Jones, Alexa Stirling, and Perry Adair, is one of the most consistently and thoroughly reticent Scots your correspondent ever has encountered.

Once upon a time I went out to East Lake—this was many years ago—seeking an interview with Stewart regarding an approaching Southern Amateur Golf Championship shortly to be played at his course; it was in 1915, I believe.

The interview was to be about the state of the course; the prospective chances; the incumbent champion—that sort of thing.

As eventually printed, the interview extended a column and a quarter in a local newspaper; about a thousand words. Of these thousand words Stewart had said three, accurately counted and carefully verified.

The rest of the words were—well, interview. I forgot what Stewart said they were. It was some expression he must have learned as a lad in Carnoustie.

So it was not without trepidation that I undertook to get from this celebrated golf instructor some of the ideas on which he proceeds with the instruction of his pupils. Here was an interview not like the first. In that it was all right (though Stewart never has so agreed) for me to go ahead and set out at length my own ideas, with Stewart saying "Yes," or in a sudden and effusive burst of confidential exuberance, "No."

Not now. Any golf instructor of the caliber of Stewart Maiden is bound to have sharply defined ideas and his own peculiar method in golf teaching. And if Stewart, whose aversion to publicity is nothing short of proverbial, elected to restrict himself to yes and no, why, there was nothing to be done about it.

I had a line of approach figured out and it looked like a foozle at the very start. I said: "Stewart, what fault do you find most prevalent in golf beginners?"

He said: "I don't know."

I said: "Well, in duffers who have played the game awhile and want some coaching?"

He said: "I don't know."

This was distinctly unpromising. "Kiltie" was as noncommittal as usual, which is fearfully noncommittal. I tried another tack.

"Well, they all have some faults, don't they?"

"Yes, or they would be playing good golf and not coming to me for lessons."

This was a sort of start, anyway. I tried again.

"They bend the left arm, don't they?"

"Yes. So does Harry Vardon."

"But he gets away with it and they don't—isn't that true?"

STEWART MAIDEN WITH *(LEFT TO RIGHT)* ROBERT GARDNER, JOCK HUTCHISON, AND BOBBY JONES.

"Yes."

"You don't bend your left arm at the top of the swing."

"No."

"You don't teach your pupils to bend the left arm at the top of the swing?"

"No."

Then Stewart, possibly being goaded, actually opened up on the topic of the straight left arm.

"I'll tell you why it is. It is possible to swing correctly and bend the left arm at the top of the swing. Vardon does it, and eases the swing a little by it. But Vardon's left arm straightens out before the club is brought on the ball. This is a delicate part of timing the stroke which none but a master should try. When the beginner or the duffer, or what you are fond of calling the average golfer, bends his left arm at the top of the swing or at any part of the upward swing, he invariably converts the swing into a chop. The arc of the club's head descends on a radius only so long as from the left elbow to the clubhead, working on a moving axis, which is the left elbow. If the axis were still, the swing would be too short and too much up-and-down. With the moving axis the swing becomes a chop. The clubhead either comes down behind the ball, or on top of the ball, or, if it happens to hit the ball squarely by accident, sends it away in a feeble and uncertain manner. That bent left arm is one of the main reasons you see duffers chopping up turf and scalping the ball all over the place."

"Then you consider the bending of the left arm the principal fault in the beginner or the duffer?"

"I didn't say so. I don't believe it is. But it is a big fault and a general fault."

"How do you cure it?"

"Sometimes I don't. I can't hold a man's left arm straight for him, any more than I can keep his head down. It's his arm. I tell him he must not bend it, and I show him how to get the club back without bending it. Then if he won't keep it straight, I can't help it."

"There's a harness made to make him keep his left arm straight, isn't there?"

Stewart grinned. "I believe so," he said. "I never have used it on a pupil. Probably it would keep his left arm straight in the upswing, but if it did that it also would keep his arm straight through the finish, and that would not work on many styles of swing, I should say. Not on mine."

Stewart still seemed inclined to communication on the straight left arm, and I was glad enough to let him proceed.

"Keeping the left arm straight automatically pre-

vents overswinging, which is another serious fault, especially with irons, and most especially with lofted irons.
With the straight left arm, the player can hardly get
the club back too far for a full shot, unless he lifts his
hands higher than his head, which he is not likely to
do. The straight left arm promotes correct wrist-work,
if not positively, at least negatively. Maybe it would be
better to say it permits or favors correct wrist-work,
which is next to impossible and certainly useless with
the choppy stroke resulting from the bent left arm."

"Do you teach wrist-work?"

"I certainly do not. I do not tell a pupil anything
about using his wrists in the shot."

"But the wrists have a great part in the stroke, don't
they?"

"Of course they do. They have so much to do with
the stroke that as soon as the average golfer begins
thinking about using them, he begins scattering golf
balls all over the county."

"Well, if the use of the wrists is part of the mechanics of the stroke . . ."

"I don't like that word, mechanics," objected Stewart.
"The best swing is the one with the least mechanics.
When you see George Duncan or Harry Vardon or Bobby
Jones swing, do you notice any mechanics? I don't want
my pupils to bother their heads about mechanics, or
which hand takes the club up, and which hand sends it
down. Both hands, I tell them, take the club back, and
then hit the ball. Leave out the mechanics. As to the
wrists and their part in the stroke, I try to settle most
of that in fitting the pupils with a grip—by the way he
takes hold of the club properly, keeps his left arm
straight, and swings, the chances are good that the
wrists being wound up unconsciously in the backswing,
will unwind unconsciously in the forward swing. That

is better for him and better for the results. Too much bother about mechanics in the golf swing, anyway. Too many maxims."

"I suppose you wouldn't even tell a pupil to keep his eye on the ball and his head down?" I suggested.

Stewart suddenly came out as an astounding radical. "Well, I wouldn't—much," he said abruptly. "As to keeping his eye on the ball, that means looking at it. I would give almost any pupil credit for having enough intelligence to look at something he was going to hit with an implement, whether it was a shingle nail or a golf ball. As to keeping his head down, I don't know whether I keep my own head down or not."

"I know," I said. "You do."

"Well, it's part of the swing, then, and no mechanical effort," asserted Stewart. "I believe a man's head flying up or his eye flying off the ball is more a result than a cause. He's doing something wrong in the swing—that's all."

"So much for the straight left arm," I said. "You teach a pupil that it is essential, and that the bending of the left arm in the backswing is the worst fault . . ."

"One of the worst faults in execution. There is another one worse than that. And then there is the fault resulting from various causes, known as the slice, and there is the hook . . ."

"The slice is popularly supposed to be the hardest to cure, isn't it?"

"I don't know. But it isn't the hardest. It's about the easiest. The hook, now—that's something else."

"Well, how do you cure the slice? And what's this other vice that's worse than bending the left arm or anything else?"

Stewart shook his head.

"The average slice can be corrected by putting the

left hand more on top of the shaft and turning the right hand farther under."

"Pronation," I assumed.

"What the devil is pronation?" asked Stewart peevishly. "Talk English. Swinging from the outside in, falling back, pulling in the hands—anything that will draw the club across the ball at impact also will give you a fine slice. If you are standing up to the shot and hitting it, and slicing, put the left hand farther over and the right hand farther under."

"So you will pronate unconsciously?"

"Listen," said Stewart earnestly. "If you want a lecture on pronatal influences in golf talk to Woods, Hutchison, or Dr. Brady."

"Well, if you are falling away, or pulling in the hands, or otherwise dragging the club across the ball, how do you stop it?"

"Just don't do it. A lot of pupils seem to think a teacher can give them a formula that will hypnotize them into doing things or not doing things. It can't be done. A teacher can change a pupil's grip so he can swing properly, as far as the grip is concerned. If he won't do it, it's his business."

"Business for the teacher, too."

"Yes. Blamed stupid business. If you think there's any fun struggling with a 200-pound man built like a prizefighter and rigid and quivering with horror in the presence of an ounce and a half of rubber, you ought to try it."

"No, thanks! There's trouble enough struggling with the ounce and a half of rubber deviltry. But we were looking for the commonest fault of golfers. A fault usually hinges on something—what does the commonest fault in golf turn on? Where is the chief trouble?"

"I suppose you'd say it turns on the pivot," replied Stewart. "And you wouldn't be far wrong."

"What if you don't pivot?"

"Then you don't shoot golf. Everybody pivots—everybody that shoots golf. There is no other way."

"But some golfers pivot more than others, don't they?"

"I don't think so. A golfer playing from an open stance has to do a bit more pivoting than a man playing from a square or a closed stance, simply because he is facing a little more away from the position he must reach at the top of the swing."

"Doesn't a flat swinger pivot more than an upright swinger?"

"Not so you can notice it. I keep telling you that all good golfers hit the ball practically the same way. And they all pivot."

"Well, Ted Ray sways along with the pivot, doesn't he? And Tommy Armour has a hip sway along the line of flight; and so does Max Marston and Alec Smith, and it looks as if they don't twist the hips as much as some others."

"The hip sway goes with the pivot, and a golfer can't twist his shoulders without twisting his hips."

"You mean Harry Vardon and Bob Jones swing the hips along the line of flight?"

"You bet they do! Where do you think all that kick in the big shots comes from? If you want to cultivate a real fault, try to swing without swaying the hips, or twisting them. If you can get to doing that—and a whole lot of golfers do—then you'll have a fine case for the golf doctor. That's one of the first things a beginner tries to do. After you get him impressed with the idea that he mustn't sway his whole body back and forth, he almost always tries to get the club back with his arms alone. That's a whale of a fault."

"How do you tell a pupil to turn his hips properly?"

I regret greatly that I cannot quote Mr. Maiden's instruction verbatim on this point. It was couched in four short words and was the very essence of pith and plainness. From it the veriest duffer could understand readily that he was to pivot at the hips.

"Well, that brings us back to the start of the backswing. How do you start it, anyway?"

"There's a little difference among good players there. Ted Ray and Harry Vardon both start the hands first. They carry the hands back almost a foot before anything else moves, even the clubhead. That may possibly be their way of getting the arc of the swing flat at the time the ball is taken, or it may be a mannerism. I don't know. Others start the clubhead back first. They say they shove it back with the left hand in control. Maybe they do."

"What's the best way?"

"The way that gets the best results for the player. I tell my pupils to start everything at once—hands, club, hips, and shoulders."

"That is, push with the left and pull with the right?"

"There you go again! There's too much stuff written and taught about 'left' and 'right' and about all it does is mix up the player. How can you start twisting or pivoting with the left hip or the left shoulder without doing the same thing at the same time with the right? Take the club back with an easy pivot and don't bother about it. When the club is back, bring it down the same way."

"I've heard some good players say they started the downward swing with the left hip."

"Maybe they do. I never watched one with a microscope. It looks to me as if they start everything at once.

Others say the left shoulder leads the forward swing. I suppose it does—it's in front, and it can't very well be helped."

"Then you are not conscious of 'throwing down' the club with the right hand, or 'starting' it with the left?"

"I am not conscious of any part of the swing after I start the club back, and I don't believe anybody else is, no matter how much they talk about it."

"You don't mean to say you hit the ball with a blank mind?"

"Yes, I do. That is, so far as any part of the stroke is concerned. If I am hitting the ball with a blank mind and a driver, I am conscious of thinking how far I want it to go. If I am swinging a mashie, I think about how far I want the ball to go and what I want it to do when it gets there—roll a bit, or stop short. But as to the stroke, I don't think about it, section by section, and I don't believe anybody else does, or can. Certainly, I never try to teach a pupil to do this or that at a certain part of the swing. Swing right, and keep your blank mind as much as you can on the shot."

"But if you're playing different kinds of shots—the push shot, the pitch-and-run, the intentional slice?"

"Do your thinking before you start the swing. You won't be likely to do it afterward. That's a common fault, too—trying to think after the stroke is started."

It occurs to your correspondent just here that this is a singularly fine explanation of that somewhat broad term, concentration. Stewart says to do your thinking before you start the stroke. While making the stroke, think of nothing but the shot. I believe this canny Scot has said something. I wonder if this can be the commonest fault—trying to think of some part or parts of the stroke after it has started?

Certainly Stewart explains unconsciously the well-known advantage possessed by the golfer who started as a child and plays the game naturally over the most thoughtful and intelligent golfer who took up the game as an adult and learned by precept and instruction. The former, taking his stance for a shot, is able to make it with a mind free of all considerations or worries except the range and the necessity for stopping the ball, if any.

As to making the stroke, that is as easy for him as wielding a knife and fork to the average civilized man—he simply doesn't think about that part of it. The latter as a rule must concern himself also about what Stewart dislikes so emphatically—the mechanics of the swing. And few golfers who learned the game as adults—Walter Travis, a paragon of concentration, being a notable exception—have conquered the impulses to diffuse their concentration on various phases of the swing.

Perhaps, too, this explains the importance of constant and patient practice; making a shot over and over. For by doing this, even the man who takes up golf comparatively late in life may acquire sufficient muscular habit, or "muscular memory" as somebody terms it, to enable him to swing "with a blank mind" as far as the swing is concerned.

"I rather fancy that correct, smooth pivoting has more than anything else to do with a golfer's position as what is called a "stylist." Surely no feature of Harry Vardon's style, or George Duncan's, or Bob Jones's, is more admired than the pivoting. It means a tremendous deal to the shot, too."

Ted Ray, not rated much of a stylist, combines a body sway with a full pivot. Ted says himself that the sway enables him to get his heft into the shot. Unquestionably he gets something into it; and his pivoting, while not as graceful as Vardon's or Jones's, is perhaps more pronounced than either, as he plays from a notably open stance, and has to turn more to get the club back to the same position.

Stewart modestly was reticent about Bob Jones's style in this regard, because Bob acquired it from Stewart when Bob was about seven years old. You may not have heard Stewart Maiden heralded as a stylist, but the fact remains that this little Scotsman has one of the smoothest and most perfectly balanced swings in the golfing world today. I know of at least one time when Bob Jones, playing a shot at a distance, was mistaken for Stewart by a man who knew Stewart before he came to this country; and I know of one critic who identified him as Alexa Stirling's teacher the first time he saw Miss Stirling swing, without knowing who she was.

It is perfect pivoting and the resulting perfect balance that enables Bob Jones to hit his hardest—which is exceedingly hard—and complete the stroke with all the ease and grace of a posed finish. I never once have seen the boy swing himself the least bit off balance, and I have seen him clip more than one 300-yard drive.

"So you think that trying to pivot in sections, or failing to pivot enough, is the commonest fault?" I asked Stewart.

"I didn't say so," he replied cautiously. "At that, I think the pivot is the turning point of what may be the commonest fault."

"Now about this matter of timing?" I suggested.

Stewart Maiden reflected.

"Well, they seem to have a pretty hard time timing," he said. "I should say that the majority of golfers never get it, except once in a while; sort of accidentally."

"Then there must be a secret about it."

"Yes. That's just it. It's a secret."

"All right. You can't keep a secret like that. So let's have it."

"It's not my secret. I wish it was."

"You can time a swing, can't you?"

"Yes. At least I used to. And I can look at a swing and see that it is well timed, or not well timed—that is, usually."

"Well, then, isn't that all there is to it?"

"Not by a whole lot. The timing device is inside a player. What I see of his swing is the outside. That's merely the result of the way his timer is functioning, or not functioning. I can tell him that he is hitting too soon, or getting his hands ahead of the club, or any one of a lot of other things he may be doing wrong. And sometimes that will help him 'set' his timer. And then, again, it won't."

"Why won't it?"

"Timing is instinctive, when you get right down to it. There's an open window. You are about 40 feet from it. Can I tell you how to throw a ball through it? If you happen to be a baseball pitcher, it would be a cinch for you to throw a peck of balls through it, one after the other. If you missed, it would be an accident—an error of timing. You didn't cut the ball loose at the right place, or the final snap in the wrist was a bit off. A pitcher's speed and accuracy both are a matter of timing. So is a country boy's ability to sting another with a green apple. It's an instinct, cultivated by practice."

"A woman would have a skinny chance to hit anybody with a green apple, wouldn't she?"

"Exactly. And it is much harder to get a woman to time a golf swing than it is a man, as a rule. Men have been throwing things around for several hundred thousand years, I suppose. The throwing instinct probably is pretty much hereditary. Some people have it more than others."

"But about hitting?"

"Same thing. I should say the golfing swing is a good deal more complex than the throwing swing; using an implement and striking the ball instead of holding it and letting it fly from the hand. A lot more complex. But the instinct is the same. And in a general way the action is very similar. Without being any great baseball fan I have seen a number of games, and I always noticed that the pitcher had a backswing and a forward swing and a follow-through and a finish that, allowing for the different plane of action, were substantially the same as in a stylish golfer. And I noticed that the pitcher with the greatest speed and accuracy seemed to be timing his swing as near perfectly as is humanly possible. It is very pretty to watch."

"So you don't believe Walter Johnson could tell me how to throw a ball through that window?"

"No. But he might give you a bit of advice as to how to draw your arm back, and tell you to throw overhand instead of sidearm; something like that. But if you ever get to throwing at all as he can, you'd have to develop timing."

"And then some! In other words, he couldn't tell me just when to cut the ball loose and just how to snap the wrist—that would have to be a developed instinct?"

"Yes. And don't bear down so on that snap. I'll bet Johnson is not conscious of any snap when he's shooting a fast one. He's just throwing."

"And the expert golfer is just swinging? Good enough. But you do tell 'em something about timing, don't you? Say a fellow is lunging at the start and getting the kick into the swing about a yard before the club reaches the ball. Don't you tell him to keep his body back?"

Stewart grinned. "No. On the other hand, I tell him to start his body first."

This was just about the most unorthodox thing, apparently, I ever heard a Scottish Presbyterian say.

Stewart knew he was administering a shock. He went on to explain:

"I want the pupil to start the downswing with his left shoulder and his left hip. As near as I can figure it, they move together. The point is, I want him to begin drawing his arms down with his hands in practically the same position as at the top of the swing. I want him to get his hands pretty well along on the swing, somewhere around the hip level, before the real hit starts. And as near as I can tell you, that is timing; holding back the hit until the body has turned and the hips are shot along the line of play so as to produce all the tension possible."

The cautious Caledonian paused, considered, and then qualified somewhat.

"I should say, that is the way timing looks to me on the outside. Remember, I am not trying to tell you any secret of timing from the inside."

I sought to recapitulate on the outside.

"Start the downswing with the left shoulder and hip. Keep the hands as at the top of the swing until the greatest tension is gained by the body-turn and shooting the hips. Then add to that the sudden unwinding of the wrists—the turn-over. Get all the spring in your system out at one time. Is that it?"

"Something like it. Then if you hit the ball on the nose you may get a golf shot."

"That's hopeful. And how many chances do you suppose there are for part of the combination to go wrong?"

"I don't know. About seven thousand. Especially if you try to think about it in parts. I don't like this business of taking a swing to pieces. And it's blue ruin to try to make a swing by sections. A teacher has to correct the outward faults that will prevent proper timing, if he can. As to the timing instinct . . ."

Stewart shook his head, the gesture carrying a

strong inference that the timing instinct, if not inherent, must be a matter of fasting, meditation, and prayer.

"When did you become conscious of a timing instinct?" I asked.

"Not yet. I suppose a man trying to play golf would sooner be conscious of not having it."

"When did you start playing golf?"

"When I was about five years old. Maybe four. I don't remember when I wasn't playing, as a youngster."

"Did you play by note or by ear?"

"By ear. And, say—that may be a sort of explanation of timing. You know some people can't learn to dance or keep time in music. Rhythm, I think they call it. Well, maybe there's a good bit of rhythm in timing. Certainly there is in a proper swing."

"Now about clubs. Some people say a heavy club helps in timing, because you can feel the head through the swing better."

"That's rot. A club should be so balanced that the head may be felt. But that doesn't mean it has to be heavy. Most real hitters prefer light clubs. The slow swingers like heavy clubs as a rule. Bob McDonald doesn't seem to have much trouble timing his big shots, and the last time I saw him he was using wood clubs that weighed 12¼ or 12½ ounces: looked rather like child's clubs. And how he does crack 'em! Not many can drive with Bob."

"I have heard that some people advocate trying to time the swing so that the maximum velocity is reached at a point just beyond the place where the ball lies, on the idea that the ball rides the club some distance and the speed of the club should be increasing after impact— that is, during the follow-through—so that the ball in rebounding from the club would get more of a shove."

Stewart shook his head again.

"Too fine a point for me," he admitted. "I think that's drawing it too fine, even if you could do it. And I don't believe one of the high-tension balls would stick on the club while it moved more than two inches at the most. One inch seems more like it. Better not bother about that. Hit the ball! If you can time your swing to deliver all the kick on that ball, you can feel you've done your duty. The ball will get away so fast it won't have time to debate with the club about whether it could get an extra yard of ride if the kick was an inch farther on. Timing is enough trouble when you are trying to fasten it right on the ball, and not some place ahead of the ball."

"So you think the commonest fault in golf has to do with timing."

"I didn't say so, and if I did, you would have what Ring Lardner calls a hell of a time sorting out the faults that affect timing. You might say that about 7,000 of the 10,000 or more golf faults have to do with timing. But there is one special fault, now . . ."

"This sounds interesting—tell me more!"

"It'll keep. It's been going on a long time."

As well as I can make out, the correct swing is located approximately in the left hip pocket, but it cannot be had in half-pint sizes at a purchase-price.

This conclusion is reached by an inverse process of ratiocination, a word I always have wanted to employ, but had a long struggle finding a job for it. I mean, if you locate the most common and ruinous fault in the swing, the thing that most surely will eliminate it logically must be somewhere in the vicinity of the secret of correct play.

Of course, I did not get Stewart to come right out and say what was the secret of the correct swing, or where it was. I may even have got an inference slightly on the bias. Stewart is perhaps the most noncommittal golf professional that ever was brought up on oatmeal. I will detail the dialogue and you can form your own conclusion.

"Do we get to it this time?"

"I should say it's time we were getting somewhere."

"Good. The commonest fault in golf, then, is . . .?"

"Hitting too soon."

"Just what does that mean?"

"Hitting too soon."

"Of course. I mean, hitting before what?"

"Hitting before several things. Hitting before the club has got back to the intended limit of the backswing. Hitting before the body has pivoted. Hitting before the hips are advanced. There are a dozen ways of hitting before you are ready to hit. Maybe more than a dozen. I never counted them."

"How do you stop your pupils from hitting too soon?"

"I don't always stop them."

"Well, how do you go about trying to stop them?"

"Depends on the way they are hitting too soon. I was just telling you there are several ways of hitting too soon."

"Is a player with a full swing more likely to hit too soon than one with a short swing?"

"Yes."

"Why?"

"Well, he has more room in which to make the mistake. I have seen players with a very full swing start hitting upward."

"Where would the ball have to be to get the full benefit of that kind of a hit?"

"About waist-high, I should say. And he would knock it almost straight down."

"Then the main trouble with starting to hit too soon is that it discharges the kick before the ball is reached?"

"Yes. All the ball gets is a hangover."

"What happens then?"

"One or more of several things. The ball may be hit square, but it gets no kick; it is merely knocked away weakly, though it may go straight. Some players never understand why they don't get decent distance when they seem to be hitting the ball pretty well. That usually is why."

"What else?"

"The ball may be smothered, topped, pushed out, swung, sliced, hooked, or schlaffed."

"That seems to be about all that can happen to one ball at one time—and all from hitting too soon?"

"Of course, hitting too soon may be combined with one or more other faults. But I imagine that by itself it could produce practically any kind of a bad shot in golf."

"That is to say, a player really talented in the art of hitting too soon could be just about as bad a golfer as possible?"

"Yes."

"Then it would appear that not hitting too soon is absolutely essential to playing good golf."

"It is."

"Well, what's the remedy?"

"Don't hit too soon."

"I mean, haven't you any method of teaching a pupil how to hold back the hit for the right juncture? What about pausing at the top of the swing? Is there anything against that?"

"Nothing in the world. Twenty years ago it was the fashion in Great Britain. Harry Vardon in his prime had a distinct pause at the top of his swing. Practically every good golfer did. The fashion has changed. Nowadays most golfers do not pause so you can notice it."

"Did they play as well 20 years ago?"

"Sometimes I think they played better, considering the limitations of the ball then in use. They played as well, at any rate."

"Well, what I was getting at was this: Wouldn't a distinct pause at the top of the swing tend to prevent hitting too soon?"

"Not necessarily."

"Seems to me it would. For one thing, the player couldn't begin swinging down before the club had finished swinging up."

"No. But he could begin hitting with his body stationary. Seems to me I told you the hit should not start until the body was pivoting and the hips moving along the line of play. It is possible that a decided pause at the top of the swing would encourage the player to start hitting before the pivot began."

"Then hitting too quick is another name for faulty timing?"

"Not exactly. It depends on the individual. I should think timing was the art of getting the right part of the hit at the ball. A player might start the hit properly and not time it right. But he couldn't possibly get the timing right if he started the hit at the wrong time."

"So the fundamental principle is starting the hit at the right time?"

"Yes."

This, for Stewart, was pretty dogmatic. Coupled with his opinion, in a previous interview, that the initiatory movement in the downswing seems to be with the left side of the body—the left shoulder and hip leading—we appear to be running the secret of the golfing swing steadily in the direction of the left hip pocket. Please understand that this is my own inference. I would not think of committing Stewart to any such incautious or undignified epigram.

Stewart added, under pressure, that pressing probably was another name for hitting too soon—"in the main." So this prominent defect also is mixed up with our commonest fault.

"Is there also a tendency in short play to hit too quickly, the same as in long play?"

"More so, if anything."

"And in putting?"

"Yes. It sometimes is called 'stabbing' the putt."

"Well, once again, now—how do we go about correcting the trouble? Isn't that fine old admonition, 'slow back,' a pretty good remedy?"

"No. Some players swing back slowly naturally and some swing back rapidly."

"There's such a thing as swinging back too fast, isn't there?"

"Certainly."

"Davy Herron swings back awfully fast."

"Not for him. That's his style. He doesn't swing back as fast as Gil Nicholls or Alec Smith. George Duncan swings back very fast, too. He's a pretty fair golfer, with a pretty fair style. At that, it might be better for a beginner to be on the deliberate side in the backswing, and not snatch the club back out of control."

"Is there anything you always tell your pupils, to help them get the club back smoothly and start the hit at the right time?"

"Yes. I always tell them to count. One-Two. Like a dance step. 'One' for the backswing; 'Two' for the downswing. In cadence, like the manual-of-arms, with the little pause between counts. That tends to smooth out the whole action and give the pupil a chance to hold the hit back until the proper time."

"Chick Evans seems to swing in three counts," I suggested. "With Chick, 'One' is the 'press forward' of the hands and hips; 'Two' is the backswing; 'Three' the down-swing. It looks that way to me."

"Possibly so. You can do it in three counts, all right. There is a little press forward right at the beginning by all good players, I suspect. The main thing is to get into a regular rhythm for the whole stroke. All along I have been trying to keep you from picking the golf swing to pieces, and you have kept asking about this part and that part."

"Well, you said yourself that the hit was the thing, and that it could be started too soon, so it must be a part . . ."

"Don't split whiskers. If you swing right, the hit will take care of itself. Remember that."

With this warning, I will have to take the responsi-bility for the summing up of Stewart Maiden's ideas on the Commonest Fault in golf, and the correction thereof.

As I get it, it is hitting too soon. Even timing is de-pendent on the proper starting of the hit; for while a player may start the hit right and not time it correctly, he cannot possibly time the stroke correctly if he starts the hit wrong. And if he starts the hit at the right junc-ture, correct timing will be most likely to follow auto-matically.

Also it seems to me that some distinction must be made in the terms "downswing" and "hit," in that the hit does not begin until the downswing is under way, the body pivoting, and the hips moving along the line of play, so as to produce the requisite tension and afford the anatomical position necessary for whipping the stroke well through.

And as to the crucial point—the starting point of the hit—it more and more seems to me, after exhaus-tive cross-examinations of Stewart Maiden, a really remarkable teacher of golf, that the hit starts as the left hip is shot forward to its extreme position along the line of play. The downswing may be started by the left shoulder, but it seems the hit is started by that little twitch of the hips which the older school of golf writers (mistakenly, I am convinced) considered as the trans‐ference of weight from the right to the left leg.

Rather, it is the winding up of the tension that then unwinds with the requisite snap at the ball.

And where there is winding, you may look for a key— in this instance in, or near, the left hip pocket.

You wouldn't Try to Play with Little Victor's Toy Clubs . . . .

Par Golf Requires
Clubs that FIT

Just swing the Grand Slam Golf Club that your dealer picks out for you and notice the difference. It *fits* you! Hit a ball with it and feel the accurate, powerful force of the contact it makes. That's what *design* does!

Stewart Maiden, teacher of Bobby Jones, Alexa Sterling, Watts Gunn and many other fine golfers, has put all his craftsmanship into making Grand Slam Golf Clubs---in matched sets or singly---in the beautiful models that carry his autograph or the serviceable models at popular prices---perfect in fit and design.

Your dealer can fit you with Grand Slam Clubs from the Maiden Chart. Go into his store and feel the difference for yourself. Also, get a copy of Stewart Maiden's new book, *"The 3 Essentials of Better Golf"* or write for it to HILLERICH & BRADSBY COMPANY, *Incorporated*, 460 Finzer St., Louisville, Kentucky.

DESIGNED BY

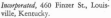

Stewart Maiden
"MAKER OF CHAMPIONS"

GRAND SLAM
GOLF CLUBS

"SHOOT THE WORKS," SAYS STEWART MAIDEN

Words of Warning Against the Policy of Playing Safe to Protect a Lead

O.B. KEELER

Stewart Maiden having reached the mature age of—well, something the other side of 40, he seems to be developing an iconoclastic habit of thought, when engaged in thinking. I mean about golf. In the matter of interviews Stewart always was on the difficult side. For a long time I had small luck getting interviews from him. Then I discovered a means of utilizing his iconoclastic inclination. I found that he was disposed to be contradictory; to bust up theories and assail conventions. So I formed the habit of approaching Mr. Maiden cautiously concerning something I didn't want, whereupon he was more than likely to get his back up and unbosom himself of the opposite idea, which was what I did want.

I remember it required four separate and distinct interviews, some three years ago, to get his idea on the Commonest Fault in golf, but when I finally got it, it was a whale of a fine idea—and the intervening interviews also were useful. That little Scot knows golf as few know it. In my humble opinion, he is the possessor of more common sense in regard to golf than any other instructor or expert I know, and common sense in golf is one of the most uncommon things in the world. Stewart has given me a lot of lectures without knowing it, and some day I am going to give them to the world. But that, as Mr. Kipling would say, is another story, or rather a series of other stories.

In the interim I got Stewart mildly stirred up by a suggestion of safety first in golf matches—I think the discussion began concerning a shot by his star pupil, Bobby Jones, at St. Louis three years ago, when Bobby essayed to fire a drive from the eighth tee over some tall trees in the afternoon round of his match with Willie Hunter, and the ball was caught by the topmost twig of the tallest tree and dropped in a ditch and Bobby lost that hole, which was half his lead, and eventually the match. I always did regard that as a rash and even foolish shot, though Bobby never would admit it, and has about got me outargued.

Without committing himself flat-footedly on the shot in question Stewart subsequently came out strongly for a policy that you might call safety last.

"I see by the papers," Mr. Maiden began, in the time-honored manner, "I see by the papers that the experts are advising everybody against trying for too much on a shot and I suppose that's what is bothering you inside."

I said no, that wasn't bothering me, inside or out. That almost anything I had tried for lately in a shot was too much. Much too much. He said bluntly that this was because I was a rotten golfer. No argument followed.

"Well," I began again, defensively, "how much ought a regular golfer to try for?"

"All he's got," was the succinct rejoinder.

"When he's down, of course," I suggested.

"When he's up!" retorted Stewart tartly. "When he's

down there is nothing else to do. It doesn't take any brains then to try for everything. To that extent the man who is down has the advantage of the man who is up. He's on a one-way street. Shoot the works. That's all there is to do."

"But suppose he has a safe lead . . ." I began.

"What is a safe lead?" Stewart countered. "I suppose Albert Seckel thought he had a safe lead over Jimmy Johnston in the Western last summer. Four up and five to go might be called safe. But was it? I seem to recall not. George Von Elm must have thought he had a safe lead over that kid from Washington—Roland McKenzie. He was eight up early in the second round. And what happened? You were there—I wasn't." I was there all right. It was the closest call George Von Elm ever had. And I never shall forget the serious look on George's keen, handsome face as he walked in from the extra hole on which he had won the match, after the grimmest struggle that turned up at Merion. Or what he said when I went up and shook hands with him and asked him what happened.

"Don't take any credit from the kid," said George Von Elm. "He shot great golf; it was a grand rally. But I thought I had him. And I must have let down. Never again! The next time I ease up it will be after we shake hands!"

I gathered that Stewart considered a lead safe when your opponent stepped up with his hand extended, and the conventional smile.

"The idea in match golf," said Stewart as if he had been reading my reflections, "is to get a man down, and then get him farther down. When you are one up, try to be two up on the next hole. When you have him nine down, try to get him ten down. Play to win every hole, right up to the stage when you may be compelled to play for a half, and then try to stick one up there for a single putt. Play for your best shot, not your safest."

"How about medal play?"

"Same thing. Of course anybody should have sense enough not to go running for long putts in a medal round—I don't mean that. Or taking insane chances after a bad shot, that may cost several more strokes. I am considering golfers who have a bit of common sense. But I've seen many a man with a good lead go into the last round and try to hold that lead with safe play and lose stroke after stroke and the lead and the tournament, simply by not keeping the pressure on.

"That play-off round at Inwood was medal play, wasn't it? Well, did you see Bob Jones play a safe shot in it? He kept going for the green on the three-shot holes, and he put the wood to that tee shot on No. 7, which would have ruined him completely if it had gone out-of-bounds, with out-of-bounds on both sides of the green and only 40 yards between the bounds. I saw Mike Brady take a fine 11 on that hole in the second qualifying round. It was a bad hole; the only bad one on the course."

"Then you think there's some psychology about playing safe shots," I suggested.

"I don't think about psychology," said Stewart. "I think that when a regular golfer plays safe deliberately, down in his system somewhere there's a sense of guilt, whether he knows it or not. And I think that guilty feeling smears a lot of shots and breaks up a lot of matches and tournaments, where the man on top is playing what he thinks is a safe game. Let him play all he has and try for his best shots. That's the way to get them."

Which may be psychology, after all. Sometimes I fancy Stewart is a good deal more than five feet six inches in depth. At that, I couldn't resist one final shot of my own.

"Even so," I said, "if I had been playing Willie Hunter in a National Championship, and was 2 up and 8 to go, I think I would not have tried to cut off the dogleg on the eighth hole at St. Louis."

Stewart looked at me compassionately for a moment. Then he said: "Don't lose any sleep over what you would do, playing Willie Hunter in a championship."

That, at any rate, is good advice and not psychological.

You wouldn't Try to Play in your Husband's Shoes

 FIT is just as Important in Your Golf Clubs . . .

Golfers who have tried them, say there's an entirely new "feel" to Grand Slam Golf Clubs. There are two reasons for this. They are *perfect* in design and they *fit*.

Grand Slam Golf Clubs---in matched sets or singly ---in the beautiful models that carry the autograph of Stewart Maiden or in the serviceable and durable models at popular prices---are fitted to *you* by means of the Stewart Maiden chart just as accurately as if built to your measure.

Every Grand Slam dealer fits clubs from the Maiden chart.

He can pick out the club that fits your swing. Go into his store and feel the difference for yourself. Also get your copy of Stewart Maiden's new book *"The Three Essentials of Better Golf,"* or write for it to HILLERICH & BRADSBY COMPANY, *Incorporated*, 460 Finzer St., Louisville, Ky.

DESIGNED BY

Stewart Maiden

"MAKER OF CHAMPIONS"

GRAND SLAM
GOLF CLUBS

MY SYSTEM OF TEACHING GOLF

A Famous Instructor's Conceptions of the Importance of Correct Body Action

Stewart Maiden

I am not at all sure that I have any system of teaching golf. I do have certain views about the golf stroke, and how it should be made.

However, I have been asked to say something about my system, and the editor has suggested that I explain something about how I go about handling a pupil who has never played the game at all, also what I do when I set out to correct errors in the swings of pupils who come to me for help in straightening out their play.

Let me say, in the first place, as far as the pupil who has never played the game at all is concerned, if he happens to be a grown man, possibly around middle age, he is usually a tough proposition to make any progress with, unless he happens to have a world of patience and persistence. I would much rather work with a player who has tried the game, for a time at least, and has developed some sort of way of hitting the ball. This fellow has at least made a start, and you have something to work with.

But to start with the man just taking up the game, I consider it essential to get him started with a correct grip, that is, correct for him. I don't know that I have ever seen a man take up a golf club for the first time, and in his own way place his hands on the club in a suitable grip. Mind you, I am not talking about the overlapping grip, or any other particular kind. I use the overlapping grip, but I've known lots of great golfers who use the so-called natural grip, and still other fine ones who interlock instead of overlapping. But the important thing is to have the player place his hands on the club in a way that will let him swing it in the way that will get the best results for him.

Then we can say that the right grip is mightily important. The newcomer has taken a grip that will pass at least, and he is now asked to swing the club, remembering that he is trying to hit the ball with the clubhead. In all probability his effort won't look much like a golf swing. If he is a right-handed person, the chances are he will lift the club too much with his right hand, and that he won't get his body into the swing to speak of. I find that common experience with most beginners.

The next thing I go to work on is showing him what to do with his feet and legs, because he's got to get them to working right to get his body into it, and he can't make a golf swing, if he doesn't get his body into it. I'm speaking of a full swing, of course.

And, right here, I would like to get away from the idea that I am supposed to be writing about a system of teaching, to say something about foot and leg action and body action, because I think they are a lot more important than any system of teaching. I have heard a good deal about swinging the clubhead and what it will do. Well, you do have to swing the clubhead, because you hit the ball with the clubhead, but I can't go along with the fellows who say that this explains everything. I've seen too many golfers get back to the top of the swing in such a position that it was utterly impossible for them to swing at all.

To make a golf swing, you've got to get the club back with the body, hands and arms in a position to swing the club down to the ball with power. To do this the body must turn well around toward the right, and the only way I know that can be done is to brace the right leg, relax the left, and turn. And the reason I spoke above of watching the foot and leg action of the beginner is that this body turning must start with the start of the backswing. If the player begins by lifting the club up with the right hand, he will never make a correct body turn, and, if the body doesn't turn properly on the backswing, there is not a chance that the body and arms will work together as they ought to, coming down.

And this reminds me that I want to say something about the straight left arm at the top of the backswing. I don't say that the arm has to be absolutely straight, but I don't know any reason why it should not. Anyway, I want that arm fully extended and firm at the elbow, because that means that the muscles of that arm and of the left shoulder are contracted, and if they are not, then those of the right shoulder will be, and it's the contracted muscles that go to work when action is started. If the right shoulder and arm muscles start the downswing, the right side will swing the club. And if this happens, the right side will swing about, toward the left, too fast. The club will be swung around too much, causing what you hear spoken of as hitting from the outside in, instead of having the body turn back easily toward the left, with the arms swinging the clubhead down to the ball from the inside of the line of play. I notice that where the right shoulder swings around, the player usually has a tough time keeping his head in position until after he has hit the ball. So keeping that left arm firm and as straight as you can at the top of the backswing can prevent a lot of trouble.

To go back to our beginner, after he has learned to hold the club right, the main thing then is to get him into the right way of turning his body to get the club back. He's going to have a lot of trouble in doing it unless he is one of the lucky few who happen to fall into it in a natural kind of way, and they are very few indeed. He just has to keep on trying until he finally gets a feeling that he has finally reached a position from which he can swing comfortably down to the ball, keeping his head in position as he does so until after the ball has been hit.

As to correcting faults in players who have been playing the game for varying periods, I think that is entirely too much of a case of individual treatment for each player to try to set down any general rule. What will fit one case won't fit another. I try to make the whole thing as simple as I can. It is usually easy enough to see where the trouble is, but it is not so simple to correct it. My plan is to ask the player to execute a certain movement that I think will automatically correct his fault, without trying to go into any detailed analysis to him. Trying to think about half a dozen things at one time will ruin anybody's golf swing. One at a time is about all anybody can stand.

The golf swing isn't a very complicated thing, but it is easy enough to make it complicated all right. Any 10-year-old boy can learn to swing a club in a very short time, yet I've seen a lot of intelligent grown men who couldn't learn in 10 years. Out of a hundred men, some will learn the swing much quicker than others; some will get to play much better than others. I suppose that same thing would apply to learning to play the piano, or to dancing, or most anything else.

SOUND FUNDAMENTALS

One of the Game's Great Instructors Gives His Ideas of the Underlying Essentials

STEWART MAIDEN

What follows in this article is offered at the suggestion of the editor (O.B. Keeler), and with some hesitation on my part, for the reason that a great deal has been written about the golf swing, most of which has been confusing to players who try to go by copybook maxims. Yet, after all, there is nothing very complicated about the golf swing. All you need to do to see this, is to look at any of the good players in action and see how simply they go about it; one look at the ball, a fairly quick action, and off it goes.

There are many ways of playing the game with satisfactory results. These differ one from another, and each may be successful. The one for you is the one that comes naturally to you. It is very hard to put in writing what players shall do or shall not do, if you have never seen them hit a ball, because what will apply to one may have just the opposite effect on another. Any competent professional can tell you, in half an hour, where your trouble is and put you to work on a remedy to correct it. But he must see you in action and watch what you are doing with the club to do so.

Here are certain points that I consider well worth keeping in mind. Take a comfortable stance, open, square, or closed, whichever leaves you a feeling of even balance. Take the club back well inside the intended line of flight of the ball, so as to force a broad pivot of the shoulders. Get most of your weight on the right foot, so as to get yourself in a hitting position, and then go ahead and hit with as much power as you can.

There are various ways to get yourself set, and the easiest way for you is the best way. Certainly nobody is going to be able to hit the ball well if he is off balance when he starts the clubhead at the ball, or if he has an uncomfortable feeling. And whatever the position at the top of the backswing, if it doesn't leave you balanced and comfortable, it is no good for you, no matter what it may do for somebody else. If possible, keep the left arm straight going up and coming down. Don't make too much of a point of keeping your head down and looking too hard at the ball. If you are in a comfortable position and go ahead and swing the club, these two things will generally come naturally.

Personally I don't think it is possible to take your eye off the ball on any kind of a long shot. On the wee chip shots it is sometimes possible to do this, but then there is always an inclination to see where the ball is going. I would suggest to every one that he try to keep his eye with the ball, not where it was, because to do this too long stiffens up the body and keeps the weight from being transferred to the left, thereby breaking up the rhythm of the swing.

A lot has been written about relaxation, and I think a good deal of this is misunderstood. A considerable amount of force is applied in hitting a golf shot, and this means there must be corresponding muscle action, which must produce a certain amount of tension. There ought not to be any tension in the muscles before the swing is started. Tension of this kind means the player is set and stiff, and can't allow the body to turn smoothly as it should. But I think maybe it will be better understood, if we say the player should try for a feeling of elasticity rather than one of relaxation.

Take my advice and don't worry too much about what your wrists or hands are doing. Get a good firm grip on the club. You can use either the interlocking or the overlapping method. I think one of the two, both of which join the hands together, should be used. And you must hold the club firmly, for you can readily understand that no one ever hit anything very hard with muscles that were too much relaxed. This doesn't mean holding onto the club for dear life so that the wrists are locked, but it does mean a good secure hold.

The hands and the wrists will do their part instinctively, if only the player gets the club back to where he is in a comfortable balanced position when he starts to swing the club down. And, anyway, any special or particular effort to do this or that with the hands in coming down will wreck the general movement of the swing, by interfering with the transfer of the body weight and by causing the player to take his mind off the main object, which is to hit the ball.

I want to add that every golfer should give some consideration to his limitations. Not all of us can be champions, just simply because we are not geared that way. Not every one can be a champion in any line. And as far as golf is concerned, it is my belief that the player ought to try to work toward good form as far as he can, but that he ought to realize that he may never entirely reach it, and that in many details he will be better off to work out, with such guidance as he can get, the best thing for himself.

THE OBITUARY OF STEWART MAIDEN

O.B. KEELER

The Kingmaker

Some way, you never seemed to expect a time when Stewart Maiden wouldn't be around—anyway if you're concerned with golf in any form. Not necessarily at East Lake, where he was a youthful professional 40 years ago; or at St. Louis for a time, between his Atlanta engagements; or in New York, where he had that golf studio. Or back in Atlanta, at the new Peachtree Golf Club.

Somewhere, and you hoped nearby, Kiltie, the Kingmaker, always would be around.

Out at East Lake, on the curious old Bendelow course, a little Atlanta kid was following Stewart around, nearly four decades ago. He was following Stewart because Stewart Maiden was the best golfer he'd seen, and the kid wanted to play golf and play it well. The kid in those days was called Little Bob Jones. And the game that led to the Grand Slam was modeled on the form brought over from Carnoustie, Scotland, by Stewart Maiden. All the world knows that, of course, and how the teaching of the great preceptor developed the game of Alexa Stirling, the Atlanta girl who won the U.S. Women's championship three times in succession, just before the Jones Era began.

When Stewart came back to Atlanta, to take over at the new Peachtree Golf Club, the oldtimers said, why, sure—Kiltie's the lad for that spot; he'll always be here.

They say Stewart died, at a private hospital Thursday. That means he's gone away ...Or does it?

Stewart Maiden was hundreds of miles distant in person from Bob Jones at that tournament when he sent the telegram with the most famous advice in competitive golf:

"Knock hell out of them; they'll land somewhere!"

Stewart Maiden was there, certainly. He was at St. Andrews in 1927, when he tapped Big Bob Jones on the shoulder, and said, "Let's go—he's in!" That was when Bob Jones was winning the British Open with a record score, and Big Bob was too worried to follow him in the gallery.

No. I don't think Stewart Maiden's gone away. And it's not only that his record in the great game is entrenched with that of his disciple, "safely and forever within the Impregnable Quadrilateral of Golf."

No. In a greater game, which we call Life, Stewart Maiden will always be around and deeply enclosed in the hearts of those who know and love him.

PHOTO CREDITS

Paul Ackerly   54, 58, 61, 65, 69, 74
American Golfer   17, 43
Atlanta Athletic Club   31 (top)
Atlanta Constitution   47 (top)
Canadian Golf Hall of Fame   14 (bottom), 19
Emory University, R.W. Woodruff Special Collections
     23, 25, 28, 41, 109
Erskine Library   78
Joan Hammond   7 (bottom right)
Kiltie Leach   21, 33
Liberty Magazine   14 (top)
James "Cam" Maiden   2, 4, 5, 8, 39
James Tingley   10, 11
Western Golf Association   iv, 7 (top, bottom left), 29, 32,
     47 (bottom)
Charlie Yates   31 (bottom)